Praise for *Visual Alchemy*

"Visual Alchemy insightfully describes the processes and principl[...]y self-doubt and making the intersection of art and witchcraft acce[...]e starting today or started ninety years ago, Zakroff inclusively shows you how to make your process and practice of artful witchcraft work for you."

—Sidney Eileen, witch, artist, and blogger

"Laura takes art from something you do in support of your magical path to an act of magic in and of itself. With suggestions on different practices to add to your art making and advice on how to turn art making into its own ritual, this is the perfect book for anyone who wants to make art magical."

**—Vovin Lonshin, author and designer of *The Book of Dream Names*
sigil oracle and creator of Sonick Sigil Music**

"Visual Alchemy builds on the basics that Zakroff introduced us to in *Sigil Witchery* in a concise and entertaining way. … This is a welcome book that provides clear, concise suggestions and prompts on how to include more art and detail into the everyday magic. … Once again, she has hit the ball out of the park."

—Ralph Victoria Young, host of *Holle's Haven: The Urglaawisch Podcast*

"Visual Alchemy provides the opportunity to create your own unique set of keys to unlock your magical and creative abilities and access magic in the world around you. What I love most about this book is it teaches how to open up your intuition visually with practical exercises and a good sense of humor. … There are concepts for makers and witches of every sort."

—Beth Hansen, visionary artist at HarmonyGoddess.com

"Zakroff casts a spell on us with her words and wisdom, incites inspiration, and teaches us that magic can be found in even the most mundane of places. She shows us the crossroads where art and magic meet, and that no matter what artistic medium is used, it can manifest our ideas into reality."

—Jessica Anderson, creatrix at Thorn & Moon

"*Visual Alchemy* weaves your style of art, your innate magic, and intuition to help you create a beautiful symphony of your creations to use every day. Laura Tempest Zakroff guides you in a clear, compassionate way to step into this magic. … By explaining sigils in a step-by-step way, you can become an advanced creator, especially when you build on the carefully created instructions of *Sigil Witchery*. Laura's teaching style is modern, easy to understand, and gives you the confidence needed to brew up your own magical system."

—**Jen Sankey, author of *Enchanted Forest Felines Tarot* and *Stardust Wanderer Tarot***

"Calling all art sorceresses, design wizards, and witch-crafters: it's time to let both your creativity and your magic soar! In *Visual Alchemy*, Laura Tempest Zakroff joyfully shares the way art and witchcraft can be combined for spells that make your heart sing. If you are an artist, designer, crafter, or just someone whose spirit connects with visual media, you'll find a ton of totally inspiring ideas, how-tos, and solid magic spells."

—**Madame Pamita, author of *Baba Yaga's Book of Witchcraft* and *The Book of Candle Magic***

"A guidebook for anyone who is interested in creating a more hands-on magical practice. It details a comprehensive system for discovering the intersection between magic and art and lays out how to use this method to get results. Laura Tempest Zakroff is generous and warm. … Her method for creating sigils is clearly explained, step-by-step, equipping you with the confidence and knowledge to create your own sacred art."

—**Dodie Graham McKay, filmmaker (*The WinniPagans, Starry Nights, Sacred Manitoba*) and author of *Earth Magic***

"Once again a mark has been made for all to benefit! Not only does *Visual Alchemy* build upon previous works, but it offers confidence-building instructions on the use and creation of art from a multifaceted perspective that includes everything from pure expression to how it becomes an act of magic. One thing is for sure, *Visual Alchemy* is for everyone!"

—**Christopher Orapello, podcaster, artist, witch, and coauthor of *Besom, Stang & Sword***

"Zakroff empowers us to craft the key to the artful doors within us that we didn't even know existed, and she encourages the reader through various exercises and practices to move past our fears and…create something that is wholly, uniquely ours alone. When we tap into ourselves, we are tapping into the universe, and Laura adeptly guides us with her signature cleverness and compassion, wit and wisdom."

—**S. Elizabeth, author of** *The Art of the Occult*

VISUAL ALCHEMY

About the Author

Laura Tempest Zakroff is a professional artist, author, dancer, designer, and Modern Traditional Witch based in New England. She holds a BFA from the Rhode Island School of Design and her artwork has received awards and honors worldwide. Her work embodies myth and the esoteric through her drawings and paintings, jewelry, talismans, and other designs.

Laura is the author of the best-selling books *Anatomy of a Witch*, *Weave the Liminal*, and *Sigil Witchery*, as well as *The Witch's Cauldron*, and the coauthor of *The Witch's Altar*. Laura edited *The New Aradia: A Witch's Handbook to Magical Resistance* (Revelore Press). Her first oracle deck, the *Liminal Spirits Oracle* (Llewellyn, 2020), has received much critical acclaim, including the 2021 Silver COVR award for Best Divination Product and the ITF 2021 CARTA award for Best Oracle Deck. Her second oracle deck, the *Anatomy of a Witch Oracle*, was released in August of 2022.

Laura is the creative force behind several community events and teaches workshops worldwide. Find out more at www.LauraTempestZakroff.com. Follow Laura on Instagram @owlkeyme.arts and Twitter @LTempestZ.

A
WITCH'S GUIDE TO
SIGILS, ART & MAGIC

VISUAL ALCHEMY

LAURA TEMPEST ZAKROFF

Llewellyn Publications
Woodbury, Minnesota

First Edition
First Printing, 2022

Book design by Christine Ha
Copyrights for the illustrations and photographs in the ten "Arts & The Craft" sections belong to the respective contributors.
Cover art by Laura Tempest Zakroff
Cover design by Shira Atakpu
Interior illustrations and photos by Laura Tempest Zakroff
The Passenger on page 61 by Eliza Gauger used with permission.

Llewellyn Publications is a registered trademark of Llewellyn Worldwide Ltd.

Library of Congress Cataloging-in-Publication Data (Pending)
ISBN: 978-0-7387-7092-5

Llewellyn Publications
A Division of Llewellyn Worldwide Ltd.
2143 Wooddale Drive
Woodbury, MN 55125-2989
www.llewellyn.com

Printed in the United States of America

Other Works by Laura Tempest Zakroff

Books & Oracles

Anatomy of a Witch Oracle

(Llewellyn, 2022)

Anatomy of a Witch

(Llewellyn, 2021)

Liminal Spirits Oracle

(Llewellyn, 2020)

Weave the Liminal: Living Modern Traditional Witchcraft

(Llewellyn, 2019)

Sigil Witchery

(Llewellyn, 2018)

The Witch's Altar (with Jason Mankey)

(Llewellyn, 2018)

The Witch's Cauldron

(Llewellyn, 2017)

The New Aradia: A Witch's Handbook to Magical Resistance

(Editor, Revelore, 2018)

Coloring Books

Myth & Magick (2016)

The Art of Bellydance (2016)

Witch's Brew (2016)

Instructional DVDs

DecoDance (2015)

Bellydance Artistry (2011)

Acknowledgments

Every successive book I write gets better thanks to the insightful minds and efforts of my editors, Elysia Gallo and Andrea Neff. Not only do they help fine-tune each manuscript throughout the publishing process, but they have somehow managed to take up space in my brain *as* I am writing. Much appreciation to all the folks at Llewellyn who help make my books a reality.

As always, much thanks to my mom, Terry Zakroff, for being a lightning-fast proofreader and my dad, Pete Zakroff, for helping to get those edit suggestions back to me.

I would especially like to acknowledge all of my Patreon supporters, especially those who have attended any of my monthly "Sigil School" Zoom sessions and shared their questions about sigils and magical artmaking. Thank you to all my Sigil Witchery workshop students (whether virtual or in person) throughout the years for your enthusiasm for the process, and of course to everyone who has believed in my art over the years.

My love always to Nathan for supporting my work by bringing me tea, listening to me rant, and distracting the cats so I can write.

For all those who dare to make art and work magic

Contents

Illustrations & Photographs

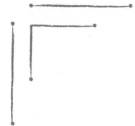

Foreword

by Nick Bantock

Writing about the relationship between art and magic is brave—witches have been burnt for less.

Every day we're flooded with images. From computer screens to billboards, we're constantly being hit with fast pictures, transient representations not designed to linger or be carefully examined. And the more images we consume, the less time we have to ponder their content and meaning. Little by little we're letting the magic of our sight diminish.

Andy Warhol knew what he was doing with his "Marilyn" silkscreens. He was making something that could be seen in a glimpse: art that didn't need in-depth observation; an icon for an icon, designed to minimize. That kind of self-conscious cynicism has led some to suggest that the second half of the twentieth century has seen commerce replace the magic in art.

Imagine if you were living five hundred years ago. Your exposure to images would have been occasional at best, so if you found yourself in a villa or church, standing in front of a painting by Raphael, you were hardly likely to give it the same cursory glance that you'd give a Marilyn. You'd almost certainly take an eon or two to examine the picture, to assess what was within.

I think we are losing our ability to slow down long enough to fully comprehend anything but bling, and that frantic pace is robbing us of our capacity to see that art can liberate us and give us a means of self-expression. Sadly, knowing that we are encouraged to have the attention span of sparrows, artists are discouraged from producing art that requires time and is complex in symbol, narrative, and alchemy.

When I first began reading about alchemy, I was confused. The language seemed evasive and elliptic. Then I began looking at alchemy's imagery, and it became immediately clear that the images were the real vehicle of the philosophy, speaking as it did directly to our visual perception. This, of course, made sense if the alchemists were to avoid the literal-mindedness of the heresy laws.

Artists and poets have always tended to make kings, emperors, and the patriarchs of organized religion nervous, with their ambiguous language and their tendency to pose awkward questions about truth and reality. It's no accident that the rulers felt a need to predetermine artists' subject matter, to prop up the status quo. Yet whatever restrictions were imposed, artists found ways to subvert those limitations. Secrets and subversive ideas could be hidden in plain sight, coded messages turned into symbols for those with a keen eye and mind.

Orwell's *1984* notes that by reducing vocabulary, you can reduce people's capacity to think for themselves. What he doesn't mention is that by dumbing down visual literacy, a similar effect can be had on our ability to be intuitive.

Magic is the learned ability to "see" that which hovers just in and just outside our peripheral vision. An artist's job is to capture the unseen; they are alchemists simply because once they are immersed in a painting, the boundary between the artist and their art disappears, time stands still, and the present becomes eternal.

In my experience, when art is restricted and pigeonholed, it wilts. All through my college years, we were heavily encouraged to narrow our "style" and subject matter, to make our work recognizable (brandable). But I found that ethos suffocating, I didn't want one head and one mouth; I wanted tongues for as many voices as there were inside me. I began searching for a means of expression that was inclusive, not exclusive. For me, the marriage of word and image opened the door to a landscape that allowed symbol and sign to wander in freedom.

Whether for the witnesses or the creators, art has always been about the irrepressible spirit of our imagination. It is paramount that we expand our visual vocabulary, not shrink it. We must open ourselves up to see, consider, explore, and create outside of the straight lines, hard rules, and white-walled boxes. Once we recognize the extraordinary power of our imagination and our art, magic will be no more than a fingertip away.

I hope you take up this book's encouragement to tear down the wall the old men built when they first decided to keep art and magic from coming together.

Nick Bantock (British Columbia, Canada) is the author and artist of the *New York Times* bestselling Griffin and Sabine series. He has authored over thirty books, eleven of which have appeared on bestseller lists. His works have been translated into fifteen languages, and over five million have been sold worldwide.

Introduction

I've come to believe that we suffer from a number of rifts within ourselves. ... There are, no doubt, multiple reasons for our sense of alienation and yet there is one that repeatedly preoccupies me. ... I tried to voice my nagging sense that we have almost lost "the image" as a direct means of thought.

—Nick Bantock in *The Artful Dodger*

I am going to share with you a secret: when I start a book, the introduction is technically the first thing I write, but it's also the very last thing I write. There's the initial idea of the book that happens when I conceive it, and then there's what happens after it spews forth from my head Athena-style. Each book ends up being both what I had hoped it would be and something I never could have imagined. I love the process and the revelations it brings.

I find the same is true for my art. There is the idea in my head, and then there's what that idea becomes once it has been brought forth into the world through my own visual alchemy.

In modern society we tend to think the creative process goes like this:

1. Have an idea.
2. Make that idea happen somehow.
3. The end result is a carbon copy of that idea in your head.

So it terrifies the bejeezus out of most of us when step 3 looks nothing like step 1. We despair, thinking we have failed, and try to hide the evidence where no one will find it. We rarely stop to consider, what if that end result is actually *so much better* than what we could have ever possibly imagined? Instead, we kill the idea before we have a chance to find out.

To me, that's tragic. And it's the antithesis of both art and magic and the actual creative process.

With each of my books, I have an idea of how I want to help others, and I've come to realize that the baseline for all of my works is a theme of reconnection. For example, *Anatomy of a Witch* is a guide to recognizing the power of your body, and *Weave the Liminal* is an aid for crafting an authentic practice from within you. This book is about discovering where art and magic intersect, but it's also essentially about how to reclaim the ability to make art. We all have the power to make art, but many of us doubt that we can actually do the thing.

I believe that it's possible to help others see, feel, and think in images, rebuilding that frayed connection to art and creativity. Through the motion of making a mark and reveling in the design process, you too can find magic and meaning in creating art.

In the Beginning

Visual arts have been an integral part of my life for as far back as I can remember. I also became fascinated with metaphysics very early on, relentlessly checking out different books from Time-Life's Mysteries of the Unknown series from the library and watching *In Search Of* and similar shows on TV. I even remember trying to master psychic abilities with my friends, influenced by the scene in the 1984 film *Ghostbusters* where Venkman (Bill Murray) is using Zener cards to test for ESP (minus the electroshock bit, of course). I think what made the greatest impression on me were those very simple symbols on the cards, and how they could be perceived by the human mind.

As I studied art history, I recognized those same basic shapes and symbols everywhere. They are carved in the petroglyphs in the American Southwest. They show up in the paintings of the Abstract Expressionists. We find them in the shapes of the buildings we live, work, commune, and worship in. They're in our alphabets, repeating in the décor found on our walls and floors, and in our clothing. They're built into the fabric of our lives. Once you start seeing those marks and symbols, you can't unsee them. Art is all around us.

Art is one of the oldest, most ancient forms of magic. Humankind creates to express itself. Music, dance, visual arts, theater—they all serve to relate the mystery and reality of our existence. Through art, we give form to the divine, share our personal and cultural stories, and interact with our environment and each other. Art is a primary form of communication, whether we're using it to commemorate an occasion or person, explore a concept or mystery, bring social awareness, or build or decorate the living space around us.

Magic, ritual, and spellcraft are also vehicles of communication. Through them, we focus our intentions to influence the world around us, create new forms and patterns, and appeal to or align with deities and spirits. A votive candle gives form to will through its color and smell and the activation of burning, and may include imagery to harness that intent. A poppet is crafted to take on the likeness of a person or animal to affect the subject sympathetically or act as an intermediary or holding vessel. An offering of curated items could be used to appease, honor, or invoke a deity or ancestor. Truly, it is the process of the creation combined with the harnessing of will that creates the magic that extends beyond the sum of its parts.

In math class we are taught that a line is a connection of dots that continues past infinity in any direction. If we consider those dots in space as atoms and molecules, we start to have an inkling of the power of the line to link time and matter, in turn describing the shape of the universe. To do this, we can lift that line out of our textbook pages and let it flow into the world around us. Then we can see lines curving, bending, and tracing around the shapes and energies of the universe, from the orbits of planets and the flow of light and sound waves to the structure of DNA and migrations of animals. Wherever we follow the line, we see pattern present in our ideas of both order and chaos, apparent sometimes on a massive scale and other times only when we get down to a microscopic level.

When we bring that line back down to the page into a drawn mark made by our own hands, it too can bend and change with our will and sphere of influence. We can use that drawn line to describe and connect ideas, goals, and new patterns born from our own minds. Whether a line is drawn as an artful mark or used to channel spirits or energy through automatic writing, scientific studies have shown that there is a powerful link between the drawn line and our memory. The drawn mark strengthens our cognitive memory and aids us in visualization. We in turn add to the cumulative effect of focusing our magical intent when we make art. The marks we make describe our world around us, as well as the changes we wish to influence in ourselves and our lives.

In addition to the apparent simplicity of a line, we can add other elements through the more complex application of color, texture, and media. A painting not only represents a person or deity but can also create atmosphere, summon a location, embellish a memory, and act as a portal. Each color that is used, every material or item included, can add another layer of meaning to the final piece, even if it's not visible in the finished product. Sculpture and handcrafted objects embody spiritual energy as well. We can touch an object, hold it, see ourselves in it, and recognize the hand that crafted it, even if it was not our own. And as time and generations pass the object along, it can collect even more energy.

The Sigil Witchery Method

In my book *Sigil Witchery*, I introduce my own method of crafting symbols that I developed intuitively over the course of my life. I reverse-engineered how I'd been creating sigils in order to teach it to others. Since then, I've taught thousands of people how to do it in my workshops, and the book has had an even further reach—far beyond what I ever expected. I had no idea how many people would resonate with my approach.

My method of crafting sigils has four steps:

1. Determine your goal or problem.
2. Brainstorm what is needed to achieve that goal or what will create the solution, listing the relevant words and phrases and assigning a mark or symbol to each.

3. Design the sigil by combining those marks and symbols until you are satisfied with the result.

4. Apply and/or acknowledge your sigil as necessary.

What I especially love about teaching, particularly when exploring the same subject again and again, is that there is always something new being brought to the table. Someone will ask a question that I hadn't yet considered. A new perspective or unexpected experience presents a challenge to solve for the future. These become opportunities for me to also learn, explore, and find ways to tackle the material. Then I can share those findings with others.

That's part of what this book is about: building on the techniques and ideas found in *Sigil Witchery* so that you can fine-tune your sigil-crafting experience. As we do that, we will also look more closely at the spiritual, metaphysical, and ritual aspects of where art intersects with magic.

Sigil magic is probably one of the most accessible forms of magic. You don't need any fancy supplies or a degree in art. You don't have to be an accomplished occultist or magical practitioner either. You don't have to believe in deities or spirits—just yourself. And even that can have a bit of a sliding scale to it in the beginning. To get better at it, you just need to practice. Sigils can help build your confidence and belief in your personal power. I believe they can also be a gateway to making more involved or complex works of magical art: paintings, sculpture, even songs—whatever you are inspired to create.

Using This Book to Make Your Mark

This book has six chapters split across two parts to guide you. In Part I: Create, we start from the inside and work our way out, learning to harness the power of our creativity. In Chapter 1: Visual Alchemy, we will explore the space where art and magic meet, why we create art, why it's powerful, and what art can do for us if we let go of our fears. In Chapter 2: Symbol Stories, we will look deeper into how sigils work, how to find meaning in the movement of the marks we create, and how to build your own personal symbol codex. In Chapter 3: Design Magic, you will work with problem-solving to refine your sigil witchery technique using design concepts. Then in Chapter 4: Ritual Application, you will discover how ritual can play a role in your artmaking, how to work with deities and spirits to make art, and technical considerations for before, during, and after the art is done.

In Part II: Collaborate, we will look at art magic that is out in the open and can help us connect with others. Sigils are often inherently personal and intimate, but that doesn't mean they can't be created collaboratively and shared with others. In fact, crafting and using sigils with others can be a powerful community experience and means for social change. But there are things to keep in mind to increase their effectiveness and usability. In Chapter 5: Out in the World, you will discover how shared magic sigils work and how to create public magical art, as well as explore ideas on how to make art outside of your personal or private space. Lastly, in Chapter 6: Sharing Sigils, there is a collection of over fifty shared magic sigils for you to explore, consider, and use. These sigils not only are a handy reference archive but can also serve as a study manual and point of inspiration.

Throughout the book you will find "Arts & The Craft" highlights. These special features bring wisdom and experiences from ten fellow artists to help inspire your path. These creators come from a variety of backgrounds and experiences and work with different types of media, but they all explore where magic and art meet in their work. Sometimes the best way to find inspiration is to get out of your own head for a bit and into someone else's! And as always, there's a list of resources and recommended reading at the end to help you along the way.

I hope what you are about to read will change how you view art and magic as well as yourself—particularly your own capacity to make art.

Part 1
CREATE

Chapter 1
Visual Alchemy

There are things that are not sayable. That's why we have art.

—Leonora Carrington[1]

For as many misconceptions as there are about magic, there are just as many about art. Yet both have been with us since the beginning of our species. One question I often pose to my workshop students is "Who benefits from you not owning your power?" I can guarantee that the answer to this question is definitely *not* you. The same exact answer is true for "Who benefits from you not making art?"

In order to get you on the artmaking path, we'll start off with exploring the space where art and magic meet. We'll go back in time to discover why our ancestors made art and what that means for us today. Then we'll break down the boxes and limitations that seek to inhibit artmaking in most people and discover how art can enhance your magical practice. From there, we'll tackle the curious nature of inspiration and ideas. Lastly, we'll banish the last remaining obstacles that may be hanging around your brain so you can start (or get back to) making art.

---

1. Heidi Sopinka, "An Interview with Leonora Carrington," *The Believer*, issue 94, November 1, 2012, https://believermag .com/an-interview-with-leonora-carrington-3.

Where Art and Magic Meet

I love a good crossroads, don't you? You just never know who or what you'll find there. Allow me to take you on a journey to where art and magic intersect. It's actually not an obscure spot that's hard to find—rather, it's quite the landmark. In fact, if the intersection was shown in a Venn diagram, it would be a colossal amoeba that covered the planet. But there are a lot of misleading signs that would have you believe or think otherwise, even though it's right there under your very feet and pulsing through your body.

I use the term *visual alchemy* to succinctly describe the place where art and magic meet. One way to define visual alchemy is that it is the magic of what we can see combined with the powers of what can we do. But what is sight? Sight is more than what we perceive with our eyes; it's what our brain chooses to relay to us, the signals of a multitude of senses sharing information, and the capacity for imagination.

In most forms of occultism, when we hear the word *alchemy*, our thoughts tend to turn toward hermetic lore and historical esoteric practices steeped in mystery. Alchemy is defined as the medieval chemical science and speculative philosophy that sought to transform base metals into gold, cure disease, acquire divine wisdom, as well as discover the secret to immortal life. But here in this instance with alchemy, we're not exactly looking for a universal elixir or a way to turn any metal into gold. Or are we? Alchemy at its core is the study and application of the magical processes of transformation and creation, imbued with spirit. With our imagination, we are able to transform thought into matter, experience, emotion, art. Visual alchemy is the process of transforming thought (conscious or unconscious) into a more tangible experience—be it through visual art, music, dance, theater, craft, etc. It is a transformation you can see, whether that state is visible in its final form of expression or in how it affects and influences the audience.

My training is in the visual arts. We tend to think of the visual arts as "the art you can see" versus "the art you can hear" (music) or "the art you can read" (literature). But that's a rather limited view of our senses and our experiences—as well as art. Some of us can see music—the words and notes making colors and shapes in our mind's eye. Some of us listen to books or use our fingers to feel the words. Most especially art has the power to make us *feel*, and that's not limited to any one sense, nor the traditional senses. You can taste art, you can smell it, you can hear it, you can feel art.

The making of art is rooted in the need to express ourselves: our ideas, our emotions, our experiences. You could also say artmaking is rooted in the desire to share those things with others, though I think the vast majority of artists create because they *have* to. Art may be classified as a form of communication, but not all art is created with reception in mind. Far more often than not, artmaking is more about the process of getting the art out of our heads.

Yet in the application of the art, when we also consider how the art may be viewed, used, or otherwise consumed, something happens. A conversation is begun. Sometimes the artist is having a conversation with themselves: we are trying to sort out an idea, give it form, problem-solve. Other times we seek to create change in our community, so our art is devised to help direct or stimulate that change, very much like how we utilize magic to influence the world around us.

An Extraordinary Correspondence

When did I realize that art was magic? And that magic could be art? It started with stories—two, in fact, that probably had more impact on my work than any other.

I was about fourteen when a girlfriend of one of my brothers introduced me to Nick Bantock's *Griffin and Sabine*. Through a series of beautifully illustrated postcards and letters (that you can pull out of the book and read), the reader is introduced to two artists (Griffin and Sabine). The whole exchange has a mystical or metaphysical feel to it, making the reader wonder if one of the artists is making the other one up. The two meet in a liminal space outside of time and place—or do they?

I was drawn not only to the mystery of the story, but also to Nick's incredibly beautiful art. His ability to convincingly depict two distinct art styles fascinated me. But even beyond that, it planted the seed that art could be a means to mystical communication in a way I hadn't thought of before. Nick's later books, like *The Venetian's Wife* and *The Forgetting Room*, also push the boundaries of creativity, spirituality, and metaphysical connections, giving me much to ponder.

I grew up immersed in learning about art history—in particular, the art that cultures have created all around the world, not just "classical" or "fine" art. I also was fascinated by the occult, mysteries of the unknown, and the power of myth. But I hadn't yet really connected the two in my own art as a young teen. Sure, I was using my artistic abilities to construct school projects and illustrate the stories in my head. But I hadn't yet made the leap to seeing my own art as something more than pretty pictures or a showcase of artistic talent.

The second story that would alter my perception of artmaking came to me when I was about sixteen. That's when Charles de Lint's *Memory & Dream* was released. In the story, a young woman artist discovers that her paintings can bring her dreams to life. While obviously fantasy fiction, the premise of the book wiggled into my brain. Aren't artists in a way truly bringing dreams to life with their work? We take ideas out of the ether and give them form. Art creates and shapes reality. If art affects the world, could I create an image that would influence the subject of what I paint or draw? What could I manifest with my work?

It might seem strange to some that two fictional stories influenced my art at such a level. But fiction touches truth. It opens ways to connect with reality when our minds or society have become closed to possibilities. Magic, regardless of how you do it or what you call it, is all about possibilities.

The Image Speaks

Another interesting connection point for me to *Griffin and Sabine* was that I identified with both artists in the story. Griffin is logical, practical, brooding, doubting, while Sabine is passionate, daring, almost djinn-like. Her words of admonishment for Griffin's fear of bridging the gap between them resonated deeply with me: "Foolish man. You cannot turn me into a phantom because you are frightened. You do not dismiss a muse at whim."[2] That last line became the first silkscreen print I ever made, the words paired with an avenging angel-like being brandishing a sword.

---

2. These words appear at the end of the first book in the series, *Griffin and Sabine: An Extraordinary Correspondence*.

I remember having a lot of anger back then, and those words felt righteous. Who or what was I angry at? The relationship I was in, my family's disapproval of it, the injustice of gender essentialism, the marginalization of the feminine divine and nature? Yes. But largely I think I was frustrated with myself, with my own fears of becoming or vanishing and the incessant feeling of needing to prove or validate myself to everyone else through my work.

The anger began to diminish as I learned not to worry about what my art could say to others or what others might say about my art. My work began to focus on exploring the conversation between myself and the art. Through my art, I could explore the divine, craft visual spells, and explore history as well as aspects of myself. Art is a bit like crafting a chat to be purposely overheard by others, as well as an honest discussion without a care about who listens in. It's a strange mix of the personal and public, being simultaneously hidden and exposed.

People tend to have a lot of fears about art, many of which are the same ones they have about magic and ritual: that they're not good enough, that the result will be less than satisfactory, and holy fuck, what if this shit actually does work? Yes, it's ironic that we can be just as afraid of something working as we are of it *not* working.

Magic starts with thought. Image/imagining creates presence. It can build a road to the destination we seek. Art helps to give shape, form, color, and direction to our thoughts and how we interpret the world around us. Essentially, art makes an idea tangible and visible. Artmaking is not much different from sympathetic magic spells that utilize ingredients whose properties align with our purpose. Just as the aroma of lavender soothes and calms, so too can the visual effect of horizontal lines and softly undulating waves. The strength of a chunk of hematite is echoed in a sturdy rectangle. Blood isn't just cells and platelets, but also the power of its red opacity to symbolize life.

Image is a direct line to thought, as well as all the ideas and emotions that come with those thoughts. Through image, we can speak in ways that words cannot express or give form to—that is, if we're not afraid to use art as our voice, to connect to something beyond ourselves.

Why Do We Make Art?

If you look into the history of petroglyphs and cave paintings from around the world, the explanations for their creation vary from "hunting magic" (sympathetic magic application or early food selfies) to "shamanistic" religious purposes. Some of those explanations can certainly apply to possible reasons why our ancestors created cave art, as there's an amazingly diverse wealth of prehistoric images, yet I can't help but remember that our brains haven't changed much in terms of size or structure since those early drawings. Science has discovered that the brain size of our ancestors reached its peak around 200,000 years ago, making its capacity the same as ours today.[3] Like our ancestors, we doodle, we tell stories, we mark where we've been, we decorate our spaces.

The impulse to create art is universal. I don't think our ancient art was a religious or superstitious by-product or something that was exclusive to a chosen few who guarded ancient mysteries. It wasn't an extracurricular activity, but an integral one. It's easy to forget that just because we have images preserved in caves and carved into rocks doesn't mean there wasn't art everywhere else in our ancestors' lives. We only have what has survived—what was hidden away from the destructive hands of time and weather.

In his 2010 thesis "Cave Art and the Evolution of the Human Mind," Martin Paul Gray explores the wide variety of prominent theories about why our ancestors made cave art. Gray provides solid arguments for why most of them don't quite hit the mark. His theory includes the idea that "cave art was a method of transferring information from the brain into the world, resulting in reduced internal cognitive load and hence costs. It also improved the fidelity of information transfer. Most importantly, cave art began a process of allowing minds to share information and ideas without the need for verbal communication."[4]

---

3. Bruce Bower, "Human brains rounded into shape over 200,000 years or more," *Science News*, January 24, 2018, https://www.sciencenews.org/article/human-brains-rounded-shape-over-200000-years-or-more.

4. Martin Paul Gray, "Cave Art and the Evolution of the Human Mind" (MPhil thesis, Victoria University of Wellington, New Zealand, 2010), https://researcharchive.vuw.ac.nz/xmlui/handle/10063/1640.

Grey, summarizing theories explored by Denis Dutton in his book *The Art Instinct: Beauty, Pleasure, and Human Evolution*, notes that "factors influencing our urge to make art include responses to aesthetic preferences, an active imagination that allows for and creates a flexible behaviour to improve survival, sociality and social status, the solving of intellectual puzzles, demonstrations of skill, power, and wealth, and also mate attraction."[5]

Essentially, our early creative efforts allowed for the mental development to receive and express ideas as well as the ability to solve problems. Art expanded our capacity not only to communicate but also to be creative and stimulate our imagination. Through the process of making art, we built our ability to share, focus, and work together in groups, encouraging collaboration that helped to keep us alive. Artmaking isn't just a point in evolution; it's a survival technique.

Gray also explores the ways artmaking has helped us develop skills that have enabled us to thrive as a species:

- Art helps us focus our attention, which is a necessary skill for learning and adapting. To create an image, you need to be able to focus on it clearly and pay attention to details.
- Artmaking helps to build awareness of the world as well as ourselves, including framing time as past, present, and future.
- To be able to recreate what we see in the world around us, we require the use of memory and the ability to recall images at will. (They weren't herding horses and bison into the depths of caves so they could draw from life, especially not caves with such narrow access that a human had to crawl through on their belly to enter them.)
- Making art also helps us externalize the brain's information so we can download or store it outside of ourselves. In turn, that information that has been turned into images can be shared as well as saved for others to encounter.

---

5. Denis Dutton, *The Art Instinct: Beauty, Pleasure, and Human Evolution* (New York: Bloomsbury Press, 2009), quoted in Martin Paul Grey, "Cave Art and the Evolution of the Human Mind," 65.

- Art sets the stage for symbolism in that not only are we creating images but we're also able to internally retain meaning and purpose for them. Symbols allow us to condense and simplify ideas so that they are easily transferable.
- Art fosters imagination and play, which in turn allows us to create new ideas and combinations through exploration. Abstraction, distortion, and stylization are the result of conscious choices requiring forethought and wonder.
- Lastly, through artmaking, we build creative intelligence, which is the ability to solve problems by imagining new and unique solutions.

But why are images so powerful? Another thing to remember about art is that the mark has lasting power and often greater universality than words. As Genevieve von Petzinger notes in her book *The First Signs*, "There is no permanence to spoken language. It is very much anchored in the moment, in the exchange, after which it becomes only a memory, one that we may or may not remember accurately, and even the memory will itself soon fade into oblivion."[6] When words and sound fail us, image is what helps us communicate.

If all of that wasn't amazing enough for you, Marc Azéma of the University of Toulouse and artist Florent Rivère have discovered in their research that our ancestors used ancient cave paintings lit by firelight basically like movie projectors: "It can be seen that Paleolithic artists designed a system of graphic narrative that depicted a number of events befalling the same animal, or groups of animals, so transmitting an educational or allegorical message. They also invented the principle of sequential animation, based on the properties of retinal persistence."[7]

Suddenly cave art doesn't seem so "primitive" and distant, does it?

---

6. Genevieve von Petzinger, *The First Signs: Unlocking the Mysteries of the World's Oldest Symbols* (New York: Atria Books, 2016), 173.
7. Marc Azéma and Florent Rivère. "Animation in Palaeolithic Art: A Pre-echo of Cinema," *Antiquity* 86, no. 332 (June 2012): 316–24. https://doi.org/10.1017/S0003598X00062785.

Finding the Golden Mean: Highs and Lows in Art and Magic

What makes something art? We can get rather obsessed about defining it so that we can feel better about ourselves. "There! I put it in a box!" we might say and be comforted in our perceived safety and dominion over art. Yet Schrödinger's art is both inside and outside of the box, nowhere and everywhere. Art laughs at your box, then doodles all over it, because why waste a good surface? But really, there is no box.

In both art and magic, you'll find folks who very much want to delineate each into boxes of "high" and "low":

- "High magic" is often associated with ceremonial practices and elevated spiritual pursuits. Some may refer to it as ritual magic or learned magic.
- "Low magic" is considered to be workings that are more earthy or natural, those that are folkloric in approach, with very little theater or dressing. The focus tends to be on everyday needs, such as healing, love, or prosperity.

Yet ritual is part of human behavior and magical practice, regardless of whether you make it fancy or not. Working with land spirits is just as important as working with deities. Learning doesn't come only from books; it must be coupled with experience.

- "High art" is art that has a curated aesthetic and is appreciated and contemplated by those with the most cultivated taste. It is art for art's sake, or pure in concept.
- "Low art," on the other hand, is art or craft for the masses, easily accessible and understood. It is art that is utilitarian and not elevated or expensive.

If you have a painting by a master that's in a museum but you also put the image on ties, postcards, and umbrellas, what makes it different from art that was created solely to adorn your dishes or bedspread? Who decides what's good enough to go into a museum or gallery and what doesn't make the cut? Is it really about how good the art is, or is it about who you know, the flash of the latest popular gimmick, or what will cause a sensation? What about art that is created to be reproduced in a tarot or oracle deck but also can hang in a gallery? It's pretty hard to tell the high from the low when you start pulling at the threads.

These kinds of separation have little to do with effectiveness, accomplishment, expertise, or power. In fact, they are rooted largely in classist bullshit and exaggerated, skewed ideas of value. The distinction alone between "high" and "low" is an attempt to separate and judge. You're less likely to find many magical practitioners or artists who use "low" to describe their work, but you'll definitely find plenty of magicians and gallery curators who are more than happy to use "high" as a descriptor for what they do. There is a clear difference in perception and attachment to the identity.

I am drawing attention to this situation because I feel it has created an unnecessary rift that is largely detrimental to our human creativity as well as our sense of worth. In reality, I think most artists and magical practitioners exist in the middle, finding a balance between work that is powerful but also effective.

It might seem weird that a professional artist isn't a fan of the major trappings of the fine art world. But the association of art with the elite and wealthy and the idea that it is a luxury has done humanity very little good. Art is for everyone. What lands in a gallery or a museum depends largely on who is minding the gates and what messages they want to send—and very little on the actual quality of the artwork.[8]

The number of creative beings who have shied away from making art because they were told or otherwise made to believe that their work wasn't "good enough" is obscene. Related to that is the prevalent lie told to young people who are interested in having a career in the arts that they will never make any money and that they should "get a real job." Yet we're surrounded by art, craft, and design every single day.

---

8. For an ear-opening exploration into art and museums, listen to Malcolm Gladwell's podcast *Revisionist History*, season 5, episodes 1 and 2.

Artmaking should be accessible. It needs to be. We as a species and a civilization need art to be accessible. Appreciation of art in all its forms is integral to fostering a healthy and creative society. When artmaking and education is taken away in schools and denied in public spaces, we all suffer. We also need to kill the false stereotype of the starving artist and replace it with the thriving artist, the explorer, the creatrix. We don't have to suffer to make art—be it good or great. That doesn't mean all art has to be happy or phenomenal. We express what we feel at the skill level we're at in the moment, much the same way we do magic for all sorts of reasons, at wherever we are on our paths.

With both art and magic, there's no "I'll just wait to do it until I'm good enough." You have to go through the process to experience the power for yourself. The understanding comes in the doing, not in the labeling. And what's amazing is that there are so many different ways to explore and experience art and magic. You can start anywhere and still find the golden mean along the way.

The Power of Art

Once we remove art from imaginary boxes that try to contain it to such things as class, ability, and decoration, we start to get a glimpse of the truth: art is powerful. As I was working on this book, the following tweet showed up in my feed: "Art isn't just something 'nice' that we do in our downtime. Art asserts our humanity and dignity, gives voice to our deepest moral convictions, and dares to imagine better futures, which is why authoritarian regimes fear and despise creators above all others."[9]

Art is perception and revelation. Betty Edwards writes in her book *The New Drawing on the Right Side of the Brain* that "drawing can reveal much about you to yourself, some facets of you that might be obscured by your verbal self. Your drawings can show you how you see things and feel

---

9. Owl! at the Library (@SketchesbyBoze), Twitter, September 4, 2021, 10:24 p.m., https://twitter.com/SketchesbyBoze/status/1434356850737172481.

about things."[10] Art helps to make the unknown known and brings attention to that which we have overlooked.

Art is change and connection. Art changes not only how we see our world but also how we interact with it. It brings forth ideas that in turn embody change in those who behold it. Art builds connections between us and the universe in its many faces: other people, spirits, gods, and places.

Art is about relationships. Art makes ideas accessible to more minds, creating a network that grows through sharing and exploration. Through art, we see where color, line, form, and concept all relate to each other, weaving together a new image. It enables us to transmit ideas and emotions to one another, across vast distances and cultures, unlike anything else.

Art is a valid magical practice. Art is my primary form of spellcraft. My practice of witchcraft informs my art and vice versa. Both words contain *craft*, which is not a lesser thing than art but an intrinsic part of its expression. As David Bayles and Ted Orland explain in their book *Art & Fear: Observations on the Perils (and Rewards) of Artmaking*, "The difference between art and craft lies not in the tools you hold in your hands, but in the mental set that guides them. For the artisan, craft is an end in itself. For you, the artist, craft is the vehicle for expressing your vision. Craft is the visible edge of art."[11] Magic emerges from our minds, and art can direct, focus, embody, and amplify that energy.

Art helps to build and improve your magical practice in many ways. Here are just thirteen of them:

---

10. Betty Edwards, *The New Drawing on the Right Side of the Brain.* (New York: Jeremy P. Tarcher/Putnam, 1999), 248.
11. David Bayles and Ted Orland, *Art & Fear: Observations on the Perils (and Rewards) of Artmaking* (Santa Cruz, CA: Image Continuum, 2001), 99.

Art …

- builds visualization techniques and focus for meditation and spellcraft.
- promotes group work and collaboration.
- aids in focusing dedication to process and craft.
- guides you to a better understanding of ritual.
- fosters connection with deity and spirit.
- helps you explore your subconscious.
- beautifies the world, which enhances your mood and perception.
- improves your divination skills.
- expands your communication skills and senses.
- develops your intuition and builds confidence in yourself.
- allows you to explore new realms, dreams, and visions.
- helps you decipher mysteries and determine their meaning.
- creates conscious working trance states.

Now that you have an idea of how art and magic work together, let's look at the mysterious nature of inspiration and how it can help you build your practice.

Inspiration, Observation, and Vision

Where does inspiration for making art come from? Sometimes I have a vision of something I wish to capture through art. Maybe *capture* isn't the right word. I strongly desire or need to take that image out of my head and create it with physical media. It's usually born of something I'd likely never observe in the world around me, such as the face of a deity, or a human heart that has become home to a hive of bees, complete with a single eye gazing back at the viewer. These types of visions may originate in dreams, during trance states, while I'm having sex, or while driving on a road trip. They are unbidden but become present in my mind, with no clear origination point. They simply appear.

But there's plenty of inspiration to be gleaned from the world around us. You're not broken or incapable of making art if you have aphantasia and can't picture things in your mind. Inspiration doesn't have to come to us in the form of a vision. It can come through observation—through any of our senses. I'm fascinated by the shape and growth of mushrooms, the wild glance of a hare, the retelling of a classical myth via a podcast. We might find inspiration in the way a room makes us feel, the look of a photograph in our feed, what's left behind in the sand from the receding ocean tide, or the texture of a manta ray.

There is much beauty and magic to be found through the powers of observation. With a vision, you're chasing an idea, often without a specific real-world reference. But when you're observing a subject, you have time to study its form, color, tone, movement, etc.

But what brings visions? Where do they come from? "How do you come up with this stuff?" people ask me. I don't feel like I do anything "special" to receive visions. Considering that many of them spawn from completely mundane activities, I could say they happen when the brain is relaxed. But they can come in times of great stress and anxiety too, although I don't think they're generated specifically by stress. I think it's rather the opposite—the brain is seeking an escape or diversion. Every single artist I know goes through the routine struggle of thinking, "I'm all out of ideas. I'll never be inspired again. I'm lost." Then they pick up a sprinkled donut, look at the colors or glaze before they bring it to their mouth, and suddenly *bam!* The next idea has arrived in a package they never could have expected.

I know plenty of folks who take mind-altering substances (mushrooms, LSD, etc.) in order to get inspiration for their work. Their work is often vividly colored, full of fine lines and veining, with unusual abstractions of bodies—which suggests to me that those substances activate a certain part of the brain that generates a fairly consistent response. Once you open that door, the trick is to remember the way to get back through it again without depending on the use of the substance. Or not. I'm not going to judge how other people follow or seek inspiration. Frankly, anything we drink, ingest, or rub on our bodies alters us in some way, and bodies all react differently. What's key is that the body does have quite a powerful memory, and we can often achieve altered states after the initial experience if we mark the gateways that get us there. I want to stress that there's no one way to get inspired, to "see" things.

ARTS & THE CRAFT
MAXINE MILLER

Belladonna by Maxine Miller (Magickal Botanical Series)

Creating a piece of art is definitely a magickal act. I have heard the expression "someone pushed the pen for me," and while dues have been paid with dedication over the years, the flow of ideas and inspiration suggests some shared credit might be in order. Gods? Fae? Elementals? Otherworldly beings aside, setting the stage for creating art is as important as it would be to collect the right materials for a spell. My studio is set up to be a magickal space, full of favored objects and talismans—I'm halfway there before I even sit down. Once the actual work commences, the intense creative concentration on my chosen subject produces the most deeply meditative state I am capable of. (Music complements the mood.) While the eyes and hands are engaged and engrossed, the mind is open and receptive to visions and visitations from spirits. And they do show up! I consider my work to be an homage to my beloved spirits, whether the subject matter I'm working on at the time is specific to them or not. The work itself is a form of devotion and gratitude for the inspiration gifted to me. I feel the connection and support of my spirit allies in my artistic endeavors, and I feel gratitude toward them when my work finds success. If that isn't magick, I don't know what is.

Find out more about Maxine at www.maxinemillerstudios.com.

You might say, "But I observe plenty of things, and I don't feel inspired!" By observation, I mean the art of careful examination—not just to view something, but to truly perceive it. For example, when asked to draw an eye, most people will draw the symbol of an eye—what their brain recalls as the basic stand-in for "eye." But to perceive an eye is to examine its shape, the play of positive and negative space, where the light hits and where the shadows sit. Rather than looking at the whole shape of the eye or falling into the trap of the symbol of the eye, you start in one place and slowly work your way through it. You start to marvel at the parts—the size of the pupil, the variations in the iris, the tiny blood vessels in the corners, the curve of the lashes. In this exercise, we slow the brain down and focus on exactly what's in front of us. We notice the details that make up the larger picture.

Think of all of the things your brain defaults to symbols: flowers, leaves, a wave, a bug, a car, a house. Symbols are great for expressing complex ideas quickly—which is why they work well with crafting sigils. Symbols can be very powerful, but they're already condensed ideas. They're gateways to delving deeper. When we observe, we discover the mysteries that are contained by the symbol. We go beyond the superficial to the layers within. We open ourselves up to receiving ideas. And those ideas *want* to be seen, heard, and acknowledged.

ARTS & THE CRAFT
RACHEL, THE PICKETY WITCH

I believe true art comes from your own magic and spirit. I grew up with the film *Kiki's Delivery Service*, and there's a conversation in it that has stuck with me since I was very little. Ursula and Kiki are talking about finding one's own style. Ursula is talking about losing her drive to paint, even though she loved it: "You see, I hadn't figured out what or why I wanted to paint. I had to discover my own style. When you fly, you rely on what's inside of you, don't you?" Kiki agrees and says, "We fly with our spirit." To which Ursula replies, "Trusting your spirit! Yes, yes! That's exactly what I'm talking about. That same spirit is what makes me paint and makes your friend bake. But we each need to find our own inspiration, Kiki."

In my experience, art and magic go hand in hand. You manifest a clay pot on a wheel or strokes on a canvas the same way you manifest spellwork. Your spirit works through you in both instances. You search within and ask yourself what you need or what makes you happy, and what your world needs and what you can bring into the world.

For a magical practitioner looking to explore art, I would look within and create work based on what you love and believe in just as if it were a spell. Your inspiration comes from what you are passionate about and what calls to you. For an artist seeking to do magic, look at your work and the emotion and meanings it embodies. Use that in your magic and spellwork.

Find out more about Rachel at www.thepicketywitch.com and @thepicketywitch on Instagram.

A Braid of Crows by Rachel Bedell, the Pickety Witch

ARTS & THE CRAFT
KERRI A. HORINE

Odinn with Huginn and Muninn by Kerri A. Horine

I have spent most of my life creating, usually giving shape and form to stories in my imagination. The process seems like magic, beginning with intent and unfolding in stages. Lately those steps are like a ritual that follows the same order. I build each layer as its own space, and I contemplate it before progressing. The use of layers has been the most satisfying change in my painting and drawing. Each stage appears as totally dependent on a combination of materials and actions. Each mark changes the work, and I have to respond to it for better or worse. Unlike in all other areas of my life, I learn through the work of my hands. Although I follow the steps, I don't know exactly what I'm going to do next. I must be attentive to the process and willing to suspend my tendency to overthink. There is a point in the stages when I know it is done, and I find that revelation really interesting because I sometimes wonder, "Will it ever be finished? I don't see how." The appearance of a coherent composition using so many materials and layers over a period of time is startling when I consider the blank surface at the beginning.

The result can also qualify as magical in that I put the pieces out into the world. Although I've done many shows, I take social media seriously as a way to propagate and disseminate images. I don't tell people much about my intentions, but the paintings are like dimensions or doors. I'd like to think the work has an effect on those who view it, whether in a show or on a screen. Overall, art has been a real respite for me from the ordinary and mundane.

Find Kerri on Instagram at @kerrihorine.

The Lives of Ideas and the Slutty Muses

For quite a few years I worked in fashion and other trend-related industries. We were constantly pressed to find the next newest BIG thing. I was actually quite good at predicting trends by what caught my eye on various travels or inspired me personally, but I hated the corporate push and copycat phenomenon. As soon as someone figures out that something sells, everyone wants to jump on that bandwagon.

But is that really how ideas are spread? From a marketing standpoint, perhaps. But I think there's something more subtle going on. Because time and time again, I have seen folks thousands of miles and communities apart developing similar ideas. The ability for a trend to pop up simultaneously without an obvious leading common influence is a phenomenon I like to attribute to the Slutty Muses.[12] Scientists refer to this occurrence in their community as "multiple discovery," though I'm partial to my term. I'm not particularly invested in the Greek idea of personified beings that bring inspiration in their respective genres, but obviously something is going on that has intelligence. It should be noted that the Nine Muses of the arts and sciences are the offspring of Zeus and Mnemosyne, goddess of memory. As we saw earlier in the chapter, art aids in developing memory and idea retention. "What is remembered lives" is a blessing that honors not only the dead but also deities, spirits, and, well, ideas. To be remembered is to be known, considered, and given form in some way. I think that ideas just want to be born, and they're going to try as many doors as possible to seed the field. That just has always made sense to me, as an artist.

So it probably doesn't come as a surprise that I pretty much lost my proverbial magical shit when I was reading *Big Magic: Creative Living Beyond Fear* by Elizabeth Gilbert and got to the part where she describes ideas as being entities: "I believe that our planet is inhabited not only by animals and plants and bacteria and viruses, but also by *ideas*. Ideas are a disembodied, energetic life-form. [...]. Ideas have no material body, but they do have consciousness, and they most certainly have will. Ideas are driven by a single impulse: to be made manifest. And the only way an idea can be made manifest in our world is through collaboration with a human partner."[13]

The concept that ideas are alive and conscious might seem weird to some people, but I'm a witch. I talk to "inanimate" things on a daily basis and commune with plant and animal spirits as well as buildings and oceans. I have sarcastic conversations with deities and create magical symbols.

---

12. We're sex-positive around here, folks, so we're celebrating consensual promiscuity, not denouncing it (with an emphasis on the sensual as well).
13. Elizabeth Gilbert, *Big Magic* (New York: Riverhead Books, 2015), 34–35.

My view of the world is highly animistic, informed by a lifetime of experiences. So, yes, I whole-heartedly believe in the conscious force of ideas and in all of their quirks and tricks. Working with them can be an amazing ride through your mind and the world.

I don't believe in the saying "There are no new ideas." I know that a lot of people (especially artists) get hung up on thinking, "But that idea has already been done." The thing is, that idea hasn't been done yet *by you*. Who cares if someone else has done it if you yourself haven't tried it yet?[14] Do we bring ideas into the world and explore them for our benefit or for theirs? The answer is yes, both, and all of the above.

A Ritual to Draw Inspiration

If you want to draw the spirit of inspiration to you, you could set up an altar honoring your favorite muse, be it one of the classical Greek muses or your favorite artist, musician, writer, or community leader. Or if you're looking for inspiration in general, you could brew a little cauldron of inspiration in your favorite mug or cup. For me, this would be a mug of tea, but you could certainly use water, coffee, or whatever you'd like.

For this ritual you'll need:

- Your favorite mug, cup, or glass (serves as your mini cauldron)
- A spoon or stirring stick
- Your favorite brew or drink

Prepare and pour the beverage as you normally would. Then grab your spoon or stick and stir the liquid three times counterclockwise as you say, "I dispel the blocks and barriers to inspiration."

---

14. Unless you're violating copyright law/intellectual property rights and are deliberately stealing someone else's art to make a quick buck. Then you can fuck right off. What we're talking about here is exploring ideas for your own sake and growth. You can never draw enough naked people or flowers or ocean scenes. Yes, it's been done before, but not by you. Not only that, but you could spend your whole life drawing a single subject matter and still find something new to express about it.

Now change direction and stir three times clockwise, saying, "I unlock my mind to new possibilities and ideas."

Lastly, change direction one more time and stir again counterclockwise, concluding with, "I open the gates to welcome the muses." Take a sip (so mote it be!) and begin to work.

Fear Is the Art-Killer

People have a lot of fears about art. Many of those hang-ups prevent them from exploring art as an outlet or seeing art as beyond something that looks nice on their walls. Hopefully I've already shown you a glimpse of the benefits of what art can do for you. I'd like to knock out any residual fears before we move on to the artmaking process.

I want you to question your previously held notions about art. Yes, art can be decorative. A painting can match your couch nicely or create a calming visual escape in a stressful environment such as a hospital waiting room. Art doesn't have to be confined to galleries and museums, held in fancy frames and placed on lofty pedestals. Art can imagine the past and document the present. It can be a vehicle for the ego or a sounding board for social change.

ARTS & THE CRAFT
K. A. LAITY

Art is often repressed in children as they age: so too magic. What came natural to me as a child—creation, trances, wonder—was discouraged as I grew older. Like many artists, I did not let that child in me die, but hid her away and continued to be true to her ways. When I learned (Westernized, white folks) shamanism, I was initially disappointed to find I already knew how to do this journeying. As I embraced magic in adulthood, I also came to hone and refine these childhood abilities.

Successful Hexes by K. A. Laity

Dreamwork is particularly potent for me when it comes to making art. It is my habit to set intentions at night to solve problems or remove obstacles and, through dreams, wake up with what I need to move forward. This was especially necessary when so much of my art was buried deep: the only art I "allowed" myself was writing.

In recent years I have reclaimed my ability to make any damn art I want, and it is often just a matter of stepping out of this mundane world into the realms between to find the missing pieces of a work in progress. Sometimes they come whole, sometimes piecemeal. Billy Martin (the author formerly known as Poppy Z. Brite) once referred to writing as falling through a hole in the page. I like to think of this stepping aside to find the art more like (as my partner Mark says) being "away with the fairies."

Find out more about K. A. Laity at kalaity.com.

Many folks mistakenly believe that in order to make art, you must be an *Artist*, as in, someone very proficient, community-lauded, and vocation-oriented. Our society's constant insistence that what you do must be profitable or highly skilled in order to be considered worthwhile is capitalist bullshit. You don't have to be an *Artist* to make art that is powerful and magical.

Another fear is that your art should clearly have *Meaning*. Not all art is monumental. It doesn't always have to *mean* something. Instead, focus on the process rather than the finish line.

Other folks fear that their art will reveal too much about themselves to others, that it will show the world just how weird they really are. I look at that problem like this: I can either spend energy trying to fit in, to be someone I am not, to make others feel better, or I can use that energy to express myself, which is a better use of my time and creativity. There's a saying that art can disturb the comfortable and comfort the disturbed. I think *disturbed* is a bit heavy-handed.[15] Art provokes thought, and thought provokes art. You can't control what others think about your art, but you can influence them.

How about the fear that your art could reveal something about yourself that you think you might not be prepared for? To that I say, as a witch or magical practitioner, are you prepared for the results of your magic when you work a spell? You're likely prepared for most of them, but not all, and if there are unexpected results, you will learn from them and adjust your approach. The same is true for divination: we don't always expect the answers we may get from our cards or stones—rather the opposite! We're ideally looking to receive clarity, not confirmation of our bias. Gaining experience and opening our eyes to different scenarios empowers us to grow and move past our fears. Making art is a great way to conquer fear. Art helps us give form to the unknown, which allows us to see more clearly. Besides, whatever that thing is that you may feel unprepared for, it's probably going to come out one way or another. Might as well be art.

Another concern is that when you mix art and magic, the work might carry with it the energy of someone or something else—whether you are buying or selling the magical art. When I make sigils or spell paintings for people, I see it as simply giving form to what that person has already established. I'm an assistant in the creation process, not the originator. My paintings of spirits and deities are not those

---

15. That's not a judgment on the band. They good.

entities themselves, but gateways to exploring them. If the buyer wishes to engage on that level, they can. Sure, each work involves my focus and energy, but I also spend a lot of time designing jewelry for the mass market. I'm not selling pieces of my soul, but simply the end results of my imagination. What the end user does with a painting or piece of jewelry is now their own relationship to explore. I do not (or try not to) make the mistake of confusing my art for me.

Lastly, there's the fear of a lack of talent, that you just won't be any good at making art. Society likes to frame talent as something amazing, special—even, dare I say, magical. They say that people are "born talented" or "possess great talent," as if there's no actual work involved, which is another lie about the arts. When you're interested in something, it's quite likely that you're going to spend a fair amount of time learning about that thing and doing it.

That is, if you are given the opportunity to do so. Am I an artist because my parents were also creatively inclined themselves? Perhaps. But my brothers aren't into art. All of their children, however, do have a somewhat medium to strong interest in the arts. The predisposition may be there, but the major connecting factor is that both my parents and my brothers recognized when one of their children was interested in art and helped steer them on that path. If someone's parents, guardians, or peers don't value art, then even if the person shows a great aptitude for drawing, playing music, or acting, it's likely there will be far less support and opportunity for them to develop their skills.

But the great news about the arts is that as long as you're alive, there's still an opportunity to explore your interests further. There is no age limit to creativity. Invest in what you value. With the arts, the return on your investment is significant.

In making any kind of art, the hardest thing is to maintain your own vision; to allow yourself the permission to fully explore a concept without compromising it or excessively clinging to it for safety. It can be so easy to sway your path to what's familiar and accepted by others, forsaking your own voice and vision to become lost in a sea of known others. Equally hard is the challenge of finding the line at the edge of creating strong rhythm and stagnating repetition. You must also give yourself the room to change as needed to continue the journey of discovering what makes you *you* and art *art*. Artmaking is not about creating art for art's sake, but creating for our own sake.

The *Mythmaker*, an Embodiment of the Power of Stories and Art to Create Our Reality (Acrylic Painting on Birch Panel by the Author, 2022)

Chapter 2
Symbol Stories

Artists revive old myths and generate new ones. Because their primary sources are spiritual, nonmaterial, they can have a clearer vision. By the use of myths, artists put society in touch with universal basic questions and feelings we all have about life.
—Audrey Flack, *Art & Soul*

Symbols may not speak in words, but they do tell a story. The trick is to figure out how to listen to them, as their vocabulary is made up of marks that communicate with our senses. To start the process, we'll explore how art and magic work through sigils. We find layers of meaning encoded in how shapes and symbols dance forth from our hands as we create them. From there you will learn to draw forth your own personal symbolic codex, as well as expand upon it while building your intuition.

Tapping into the Matrix: Another Way of Thinking about How Sigils Work

In *Sigil Witchery*, I explain how the drawing process helps us access the higher cognitive thinking centers in the brain that aid in memory, comprehension, and visualization. I also include a cursory exploration of magic. For this book, we're about to go conceptually deeper when considering how sigils and magic work.

Let's start with sympathetic magic. Sympathetic magic pulls upon associations and connections, whether it's "like affects like," microcosm-macrocosm interaction, or established relationships of other kinds. The folklore says this is true about X plant or Y stone, and enough people have believed in the association that a link has been created. There's often some sort of initial connection that sparked that folklore, but not everything is rooted in something practical or chemically true. Sometimes associations happen through misinformation—for example, a word that's misspoken, misheard, or misread. That altered word can stick and become part of the culture, taking on another meaning. Mistakes can charm us and take on a whole new life. What matters in the end is that when we think/use/say a certain thing, it creates a visual or mental association that our brains respond to. The ingredients become stepping-stones to creating that bigger picture.

In my method of crafting sigils, the brainstorming process is where the heavy lifting of the magic happens. Those brainstormed elements are the ingredients of your spell that help you visualize the outcome. They are the general map to where you want to go. When you associate them with marks, you are essentially marking the route to that destination in such a way that your brain kicks into gear. Magic starts with thought, and the more specific those thoughts can get to help in the picturing process, the more direct the route can become.

The sigil is the combined result of those thoughts and your focus. It's like crafting a key to a door you didn't even know existed but just now located. But how do you know that sigil is the right one? What does it mean when your brain has that recognition of "Ah, this is good! Yes, make it so!"

Well, consider roads and routes. To be able to navigate a path, you need to be able to drive or tread upon it, follow the signs, and have the gas and/or necessary supplies to help get you there. That means clearing the way, knowing the markers, and being prepared. There are certain elements that make up a good road or trail versus one that's harder to navigate. You've done the work, so it's easier to recognize the path before you.

The other way of looking at it is a bit more mystical yet also scientific. The universe is made up of shapes. From subatomic particles and cells to light waves, fractals, and galaxies, everything has a structure. We often use those structures to help identify associations, like "this flower looks like a lung, therefore it may help with lung ailments," and sometimes it actually freaking does! Everything around us and in us has a pattern.

How Pattern, Shape, and Mathematics Work with Metaphysics

Geometry, as we typically experience it in school, doesn't seem like it has many real-world applications as we are given formulas to memorize about calculating circumference and cosine. Yet geometry is a means to describe the shape and structure of the universe. Circles, triangles, and hexagrams are models we use as a guide. But on a deeper level, the universe is much more organic, rhythmic, and patterned than basic geometry would lead us to see. What may seem random in nature is actually part of a larger (and smaller) pattern. The shape and distribution of a plant's leaves is influenced by its cellular structure, which is determined by its DNA, which is made up of protein molecules constructed of atoms and subatomic particles, as well as the space between all of these elements.

In the Sigil Witchery method, we use shapes, lines, and other marks to symbolize what we seek to accomplish. Numbers come into play, helping to create both meaning and pattern. It is possible to conceive that the resulting sigil is akin to a fractal—part of a pattern locking into a greater solution. Another reason why this method may work so well is that we are subconsciously keying into the pattern of the universe we are seeking to influence. Our brain recognizes the shape and sets the equation into motion. The sigil matches or locks into the desired pattern, creating a connection.

Motifs and patterns make us feel things—safe, excited, anxious, relaxed—all depending on the components they're made up of and how they're arranged in space. The patterning chains of proteins, the repetition of cells in our bones and muscles, and the spiraling collection of genes in our DNA all determine the function, shape, and design of our bodies. Symbols and marks key into and unlock the structure of the universe. Is this theory profoundly mystical? Maybe, but as an artist and someone who observes nature and science, it doesn't seem too strange to me that crafting symbols is a means of linking into the patterns of the universe in a way that gives us a little more control. It's an opportunity for us to become part of the story, and maybe even narrate it.

The Story of the Symbol

I've come to realize that my brain works best by telling stories. When I'm creating art, I'm telling stories. I'm thinking not only about the depiction of the subject matter but also of how the marks and colors form a relationship. I'm telling a story to myself, to the viewer, to the materials themselves. The same is true of dance. I ask myself what story the music is telling and how I could best translate that through my body. Even in something as "non-artistic" as math, I'm considering the relationships of the numbers. What is the process of how they go there or how they combine? What relationship is being explained or related by the numbers and symbols?

Our brains process things differently, so you might not think in stories like me, but I do tend to think our brains are wired for stories. That's why myths, fairy tales, and ghost stories are so intriguing and so enduring. The stories we tell our children have underpinnings of morals, ethics, and problem-solving skills. Stories transmit those ideas more effectively than rules. As Brian Boyd, a Distinguished Professor at the University of Auckland in New Zealand, explains in his book *On the Origin of Stories*, "Fiction, like art in general, can be explained in terms of cognitive play with pattern—in this case, with patterns of social information—and in terms of the unique importance of human shared attention."[16] Stories hold our attention more effectively, fostering an emotional response that builds conceptual relationships.

When I read the tarot for someone else, I often turn to stories to help them relate better to what's going on. The average person isn't likely to know the symbolism behind the Seven of Swords, but if I explain the situation with a metaphor or myth, they suddenly see where they are in the story.

Story is part of the weaving process, bringing together the elements that craft the larger pattern. Stories give us place, time, meaning, and emotions. If we look at symbols as elements in a story, we relate more deeply to them. Where does this character go in this situation? How does it need to change? How does it relate to this other character? Like an actor, it can take on different roles while maintaining the same general appearance.

---

16. Brian Boyd, *On the Origin of Stories* (Cambridge, MA: Belknap Press of Harvard University Press, 2009), 130.

The story doesn't have to be complex, with an elaborate backstory and character motivation. Rather it's more like a snapshot or short little chat that gives us a glimpse into what is possible. Let's take three different shapes—a circle, a horizontal line, and a crescent moon—and consider how their meanings can change depending on the story we wish to tell.

A Circle, a Line, and a Crescent Moon

Here are the meanings of the individual symbols on their own:

Circle: community, full moon, container, deity, wholeness

Horizontal Line: baseline, ground, minus, border, step, road

Crescent Moon: basket, waxing or waning (increase or release), horns, crown, reaching

Here are just five possible scenarios for a composition using these three symbols:

1. The circle sitting on top of the line, with the crescent on top facing up
2. The circle sitting on top of the line, with the crescent on the bottom facing down
3. The line bisecting the circle, with a crescent on the top and the bottom
4. The line bisecting the circle, with a crescent on either side
5. The line placed through the bottom third of the circle, with the crescent inside the circle

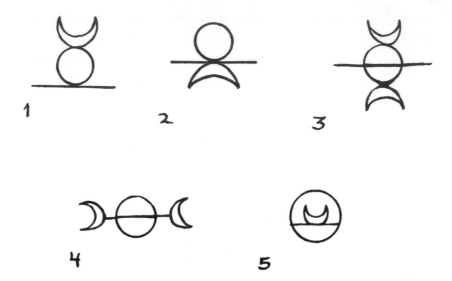

Five Possible Scenarios for a Composition Using the Same Three Symbols

Now let's consider what each of these scenarios could mean. Note that each story is simply a possibility, not the definitive one.

1. *Smooth rolling:* The circle represents community being on a strong foundation, able to move in a variety of directions smoothly. The crescent on top represents gathering resources while also being protected. Wherever the community goes, the crescent moves with it, staying on top.

2. *Balance and refinement:* This grouping feels like our circle trying to achieve a sense of balance. The crescent is working as a release valve (to let go of something unwanted) but also suggests mobility, with the points of the crescent acting like feet. The line can be arms reaching outward or can represent an equation, reducing something to its essential parts.

3. *Meet in the middle:* Here we're reminded of the classic "triple moon" imagery, representing the waxing, full, and waning moons, but they're aligned vertically instead of horizontally. Here the top crescent is bringing in what is desired, while the bottom crescent releases what is no longer needed. The line in the center creates a barrier or marking point—our circle is half-empty, half-full. The line could also represent reaching out, trying find a center of balance.

4. *Message in (or out):* Here the triple moon is situated in the traditional horizontal fashion, but the centralized horizontal line creates three interlinking elements. The waxing and waning moons reach outward. They could be listening and pulling information in toward the center, or they could be speaking out and directing that information away from the core.

5. *Staying afloat:* Here there are several subtle factors at play. There is a change of scale in the crescent, and it has been moved inside the circle. The line is placed toward the bottom of the circle instead of through the center. The smaller crescent looks like a boat sailing on the surface of the water, and the circle becomes a moon or sun surrounding and reflecting the boat. We could see the crescent as our hopes and aspirations being placed on a calm sea and encircled with protection.

There are many other compositions and related stories we could come up with, but this should give you a solid sense of the variety that is possible with just a few basic symbols and how they are oriented to each other. Remember, there is no one true interpretation. The Austrian artist Gustav Klimt is widely attributed to have said "Art is a line around your thoughts." Your thoughts and resulting interpretation of what you experience is the root of your art and its meaning.

Movement of the Marks

How do I decide what a mark means? I consider the movement involved in making the mark, as well as the overall visual effect and feeling I get from looking at it. This helps me create the story I wish to tell. After reading the following section, you'll be able to understand how to find the movement of the marks for your own work.

The Shape of Movement

In chapter 2 of *Sigil Witchery*, I introduce a variety of common marks and symbols that can be utilized for creating sigils. For each one, I share some interpretations and possible meanings, and often talk about the energy of the mark.

Many people just want to know what a mark means, so they can use it. But why or how does a mark have a certain meaning? The answer is often in how the mark is made and the visual impression it gives once completed. Furthermore, if you understand *why* a mark or symbol has a certain meaning, you'll be able to use it more successfully.

Many marks and symbols are universal in their appearance, if not their precise meaning. There's a reason that you'll find similar marks and symbols all across the world. Actually, there are several important reasons:

1. We have a common ancestry. While meanings of marks can and will differ across cultures, generations, and platforms, there's a part of our DNA that recalls when we made the first marks thousands upon thousands of years ago.
2. Humans draw what they perceive in the world around them. We have a natural curiosity to discover and mimic movement as children. Presented with paint or markers, we will make dots, lines, swirls, circles, crescents, triangles, dashes, zigzags, and crosshatches without much thought. Whether it's the entoptic phenomenon arising from our minds or the patterns present on our clothes, walls, or flora and fauna, we are drawn to create them. They are the basic building blocks of life, the universe, and motion.

3. These marks fascinate our brains, and we recognize the feel of them as we draw them with our bodies. A mark is the capture of energy in motion—like a photograph. It's a way to express ourselves that is commonly understood on multiple levels.

4. As a species, we love to see what our neighbors and friends are up to, as it's an ingrained survival technique. Shared communication can mean shared survival, as well as learning new and better ways of doing something. In healthy cultures, the information flows both ways.

5. Similar marks are found across cultures around the world due to the phenomenon of multiple discovery, aka the Slutty Muses.

With all this in mind, remember that what a mark means ultimately depends on you. Your personal experience plays the largest role in creating meaning. All you have to do is look at the cross-hatch mark to see how age, background, and experience affect its meaning. To your grandparent, it's a pound sign. To a child, it's a tic-tac-toe board. To a musician, it's a sharp sign. And thanks to the internet, most people now recognize it as a hashtag.

But before we get into the meaning, take some time to discover the movement of the marks with the following exercises.

Draw the Music

For this exercise you will need a sizable newsprint pad (at least 14-by-17 inches), a fresh chunky marker (ideally nontoxic), and access to music.

I teach a dance intensive called "Museum Quality Dance." In it, I use visual art techniques to help dancers create more artful and inspired dances. One of the exercises we do involves giving the dancers large pads of newsprint paper and markers. Then I put on different kinds of music and ask them to draw what they hear using lines and marks but no identifiable images. If there's a pause or break in the music, they can either stop or lift their marker off the paper. They might draw swirly lines for a violin solo or sharp, short marks for a syncopated drum feature. Maybe there's a repeating motif for a melody that comes back again and again. For the dancers, this gives them a visual cue as to what the music looks like, and then in turn how to translate it to their bodies. Music stops? Time for them to pose or pause their movements. Swirly violin might translate into arm undulations or spiraling chest or wrist circles. This practice helps them learn to listen to the music more closely and decide what movements best fit the music. It also builds their improvisational skills.

While you could also use this exercise to find movements for sigil-related dances, my suggestion here is to put on a song and do the drawing part of the exercise. If it's a song you know really well, be sure to actually listen to it, rather than anticipating what's coming next. You could choose a song you've never heard before, but it helps to have at least a little bit of an emotional connection to the song so you can also factor feeling into your mark making.

Be in the moment and see what flows through your marker. Using a chunky marker is especially helpful so you can clearly see the marks you have made. A pencil or finer marker may run out, break, or be difficult to see. What this exercise does for the sigil maker is help you pull from your brain shapes and lines based on what you hear—be it lyrics, rhythm, or melody. Unlike the dancers, you can choose to draw more recognizable shapes, but be sure to avoid making actual images or scenes. You're not drawing a landscape or making a portrait; you're pulling out shapes and marks inspired by the music. You also don't want to spend a lot of time drawing one shape and making it perfect. You should keep moving with the music. The result will likely be messy, though it helps if you work in stanzas, filling up the paper in serpentine lines. That way you can play the song and go back over what you've drawn to see correlations.

Music and Gesture Drawings from One of the Author's Dance Workshops

The Feeling of the Marks

To the average person, a dot is just a dot, right? No big deal. Or is it? In writing, the dot of a lowercase *i* and a period are essentially the same mark. But they feel slightly different when we write them. The *i* tends to be quick and light, while the period often gets more pressure and weight. Their positioning also clearly affects their meaning. This subtle distinction of feel is not just true in drawing but can also be felt when typing various punctuation marks and characters. When I type a period, the stroke is rarely made by itself; rather, it is immediately followed by a tap on the space bar or the return key. To make an uppercase *I*, the shift or caps lock key must be used. When we become skilled at typing, we don't really think about it. But when we first start learning how to draw letters or type properly, we are much more aware of what our hands are doing.

Much of the nuance and meaning of each mark can be distilled in the process of drawing it. A soft-leaded pencil, like an ebony or a 6B, gives a smooth feeling, while a marker with a spongy tip gives a bounce. A ballpoint pen has a roll to it. The feeling of every mark you make is amplified by the tool. How long you make contact with the paper and how much pressure or force you use both affect the mark-making experience.

To get a sense of how marks feel as you make them, get out a blank sheet of paper and a ballpoint pen. (You can also try this again with a soft pencil or marker to get a sense of how the tool affects the drawing.)

- Draw a dot. Just make a simple point, one quick mark, on the surface of the paper. Next, spend a little more time making the dot, allowing it to stand out on the page like it has a purpose. Then draw a tiny circle and shade it in. Make a row of four dots quickly. Notice how each mark-making has a different movement to it.

- Draw a short horizontal line, like a minus sign. Make multiple dashes of a similar size in a row. Draw an equal sign. Now make one long horizontal line. Again, they are all the same basic mark, but the length and repetition make a difference in how each one feels as it's being drawn.

- Draw a vertical line about one inch long. Make four more of them next to each other. Now draw five horizontal lines across and perpendicular to the vertical lines. Make a single plus sign, then a hashtag. Feel the difference between the singular intersection and the multiple connection points.

- Draw a short diagonal line. Draw another one facing the opposite way. Make four more companion marks in a row on either side of the first two. Make a zigzag by alternating each one. Make chevrons by themselves, pointing up, down, left, and right.

- Draw an *X*. Now make three of them next to each other. Are you making each line from the bottom up, from the top down, or from both directions? Try to do each consciously. Make an asterisk by drawing an *X* and a plus sign together.

- Draw a square in one continuous mark. Starting at the bottom-left corner, draw up, go across, draw down, and return to where you started. Trace over the square you just made, paying attention to the sharpness of the corners and the parallel lines. Try the same with a horizontal and a vertical rectangle.
- Draw a circle. Try to trace around it again and again clockwise without stopping as you make each revolution. Reverse direction and draw the circle counterclockwise.
- Draw a figure eight upright and another lying horizontal. Trace over each design and try changing direction at the center.
- Draw a wavy horizontal line. Draw another one immediately below and above it, mimicking the same wave. Now do the same with vertical wavy lines. Try making one with big waves and another with very small waves.
- Draw a spiral, starting with a dot in the center and expanding out. Now trace that same spiral traveling from the outermost point back to the center dot, then reverse and trace it again moving outward.

You can approach any mark or symbol this way, carefully exploring the feeling of its shape. Consider: Is the shape open or closed? How would something move inside or around this shape? What happens when you multiply the shape or mirror it? These considerations might not seem like a big deal, but every mark is made with movement. When you are able to connect ideas, feelings, and sensations to those movements, marks suddenly take on more personal meaning. You are building a relationship with each mark and recording it through the drawing process—not only on paper, but in your memory as well.

None of the marks in this exercise should be unfamiliar to you, but through this contemplative drawing process, they can certainly become more familiar. The marks are entering into your personal catalog of marks with meaning.

Creating a Personal Symbolic Language

We all have a personal alphabet of symbols and marks, but some of us have a harder time recognizing and accessing it. I myself am pulling from decades of visual associations built out of my art school training and the personal mythology I've created through my work. To be clear, I'm not talking about replacing the letters of your language with a whole other set. Instead, this is a codex of marks and symbols that have meaning *for you*.

For many people, the symbol/mark recall gets easier with time and practice, but others find they still have a mental block. Creating a personal symbol codex can give you a handy reference tool to refresh your brain. Unlike an established alphabet, this personal one can change and morph over time. You might find better symbols you prefer down the line or discover that your relationship with a particular mark has changed. These changes and additions don't invalidate the older sigils you have made, but simply become ways to refine your technique for future sigils.

To build a physical codex to record and later reference, you can start with common words or phrases and contemplate what marks could be used to represent them in symbolic form. If you have a magical focus that you specialize in (such as healing or protection magic), it's probably more helpful to make a list of your most frequently used words and phrases, depending on the scenarios that you encounter the most.

You could also start with a set of symbols that you are most drawn to and determine what they mean to you. A great starting place is the collection of thirty-two signs catalogued by Genevieve von Petzinger, which can be easily searched online and seen in her TED Talk.[17] These marks are our most ancient ones and have appeared all over the world. Record the ones that stand out to you the most and consider what they can mean. Add other marks and symbols that you have a relationship with as you recall them.

---

17. View Genevieve von Petzinger's 32 signs here: Patrick d'Arcy, "What the Mysterious Symbols Made by Early Humans Can Teach Us about How We Evolve," Ideas.ted.com, June 7, 2017, https://ideas.ted.com/what-the-mysterious -symbols-made-by-early-humans-can-teach-us-about-how-we-evolved/.

I can't emphasize enough that it's unlikely you'll be able to sit down and create a whole alphabet out of nothing in a single sitting. It takes time to build up a comfortable symbol vocabulary that is efficient and memorable. Acquiring an intuitive familiarity with something you've created also requires usage. There's creating the design and then there's the actual process of living the design. It's a bit like writing song lyrics—they may sound good on paper, but until you actually sing them, you won't know how easily they roll off your tongue.

You can also create your own personal color chart, as colors certainly hold symbolic meaning. New magical practitioners are often in search of the definitive chart of "what color of candle do I need for this spell?" I recommend you set aside that Tumblr color correspondence chart and consider your own feelings instead. No offense to my friends who make amazing and fabulous candles, but color meaning depends so much on both personal and cultural associations. Red can mean love, anger, blood, vitality, fortune, fertility, family, or passion, depending who you ask and where you are in the world. If you have a very negative association with a certain color, it's going to be hard for you to see it as anything but that, despite Big Witch Candle Mart telling you that's the color you *must* have for your spell to work.

While it might seem like a daunting task to create a personal symbolic codex, remember that you don't have to do it all at once. The chart will not only help you establish your own system of marks and symbols but will also be a wonderfully handy (and beautiful) thing to have in your grimoire or book of shadows.

A Chart of My Personal Symbol Codex Inspired by the Tarot

fool	magician	priestess	empress	emperor
hierophant	lovers	chariot	strength	hermit
wheel of fortune	justice	hanged man	death	temperance
devil	tower	star	moon	sun
judgment	world	wand	cup	coin	sword

Expanding Your Marks and Symbols: How to Refresh Your Brain

Say you've been using the Sigil Witchery method for a while now and you feel like you're using the same marks and symbols again and again. Well, on one hand, that's not really a bad thing, because as long as the marks you assign to a word make sense, you're on point. But sometimes it's more about digging a little deeper in your consciousness to overcome blockages, be they spiritual, mental, emotional, or even physical. Often this dissatisfaction comes from our association with a word or the fact that it doesn't quite express the meaning of the idea we've trying to convey. This is where checking a thesaurus (like thesaurus.com) can come in handy.

For example, imagine you're working on creating a sigil to help bolster your career so that you're making new contacts and getting new opportunities. You've written down the word *growth*, and the only mark you can think of to represent it is an upward arrow—which doesn't quite seem to express what you're looking for. You're not looking for upward mobility in this case, but rather to expand. Looking up *growth* on thesaurus.com yields *advance, improvement, prosperity,* and *success* in the first row, but then you see the words *cultivation, flowering, proliferation, sprouting,* and *stretching*. Now, instead of an upward arrow, you begin to picture something more plantlike: a vine, a flower, a bud, roots spreading out, etc. This is closer to what you initially had in mind when you wrote down *growth* but couldn't quite put your finger on why it wasn't quite enough.

Occasionally our brain just wants to reach for whatever is closest, but it doesn't take much to push the thought process a little further and get the creative juices flowing. In addition to trying the thesaurus, you could also enter your initial word into a google image search and see what you get.

It's not cheating to switch things up so you can find a better solution. What you're *not* doing here is finding random images or symbols that you've never worked with before and shoehorning them. You can, of course, add new marks and symbols as you learn about them, but be sure to spend the time necessary to build a connection. More often than not, images found online are misappropriated, unsourced, or misexplained (especially on Pinterest). If you are drawn to a symbol you find online, you can use an image resource such as TinEye.com to see if you can find other sources and information about the symbol. Find out where it came from, who made it, what it's used for, and possible alternative meanings.

Trusting Your Intuition

Most new magical practitioners tend to disregard their intuition in favor of something "established," meaning a spell or sigil that someone has already created, rather than trusting in something they themselves create. There's nothing wrong with going with a tried-and-true charm, especially when you understand how and why it's used. But a lot of spells in books and online lack context or practical application. Sigils that were created by someone else with a very personalized focus will likely not be aligned with how you'd best wish to achieve your goal. For example, you might come across "A Love Sigil" on Tumblr that's just an image with that title. What kind of love was the creator referring to? Is it for self-love, a romance, or a steamy one-night stand, or to draw love in general to the user? In this case, you're better off creating a sigil that suits your own personal needs and goals. When it comes to the shared magic sigils in chapter 6, you can see exactly what went into each sigil and consider whether that aligns with your goals. You might even be inspired to use part of one as a base and build upon it. Either way, you'll have a better understanding of what you're using and why.

The more you learn to trust yourself, the better and more effective your practice will become. You are building a personal vocabulary, an arsenal of wisdom, a cabinet of curiosities to pull upon whenever you need them. How you see and use certain marks and symbols can be unique to your understanding—and therefore far more likely to work better for your specific issues and goals. Symbols and marks may be ubiquitous across cultures, but it's your own personal experience and understanding that will help build a frame of reference that makes sense to you.

Before we move on to design, consider the following quote from Brian Boyd: "Art builds our confidence, at the individual and the group levels, in shaping our destinies."[18]

You can do the thing.

---

18. Boyd, *On the Origin of Stories*, 124.

Chapter 3
Design Magic

To practice any art, no matter how well or badly, is a way to make your soul grow.
So do it.

—Kurt Vonnegut[19]

In this chapter you'll find design components that can help increase the effectiveness of your sigils and aid you in becoming more comfortable with the design process. It might seem like artists have a natural sense of design and composition, but the truth is that anyone can learn to train their brain to get a better sense of what works and what doesn't. While some of us have a predisposition to what others may label as "talent," that innate sense really comes through practice, experience, and observation. Dedicating time and thought goes a long way in building design muscles. Practice comes from experience, which is found in the doing—participation in the process.

Process is how something is created. Some creation methods are subtractive in nature, while others are additive. Others mainly rearrange existing elements into a new order. They're all valid in their own way. The popular chaos magic sigil-making method where you eliminate duplicate consonants and remove any vowels is a bit like sculpting marble or wood. You start with a block of

---

19. Kurt Vonnegut, excerpt from remarks made onstage at the University of Wisconsin in Madison on the evening of September 22, 2003, https://inthesetimes.com/article/knowing-whats-nice.

a larger idea and chisel it down to the idea you have in your mind's eye. The Sigil Witchery method is more like building a painting or creating a matrix for printmaking. You take the raw materials and construct them into something more refined, adding layers. Whether the work is for your own eyes only or is made to be replicated for others to use, you're creating by design.

At the heart of design is problem-solving. Much of the following material focuses on troubleshooting techniques that will assist you in navigating some of the most common problems and questions I've heard from other magical practitioners. You might think you're the only one struggling with an issue, but chances are, if you're having difficulty, there are many other people in the same boat. The most important thing is to experiment with ideas and see what happens. You can read about art and magic all day long, but it's a whole other animal to make the leap to actually doing it. Most importantly, have some fun doing it!

Start Here or There? Creating and Copying Details

For some folks, one of the most difficult parts of creating a sigil is choosing which mark to start with. They ask, "Does it matter what element you start creating a sigil with? How do you choose the right one?" Similarly, with sigils that are meant to be shared, people may be unsure of where in the design they should begin when replicating it.

For the majority of sigils I create, I either follow my intuition or look at the brainstormed list of words and assigned symbols to see what marks show up repeatedly. If a circle shows up more than any other shape or mark, that's likely the best place to start drawing. If a symbol or shape has significant meaning for the person the sigil is for, I may start with that. Maybe there's one word or element that really is the key factor for the sigil, in which case it's a good idea to start with that as the foundation. Another option is to start with your large or dominant shapes, then work your way through to the smaller ones. Really, there is no wrong place to start when you're designing a sigil. It's not going to self-destruct if you choose the wrong order when figuring out how the thing should look, especially since you might be trying out several or a dozen variations until you find the overall design you like the most.

You could also have an evolving sigil for a working where every day, week, or moon you add another layer to the sigil. The Sevenfold Waning Moon Spell on my Patheos blog allows for the participant to focus on one aspect of the overall design at a time, depending on how they wish to approach the spell.[20] Another example would be if a coven creates a sigil for their group to mark and honor a member's progress. Let's say their tradition has five levels of initiation or degrees. At the first level, the initiate is introduced to the first element of the sigil. Then at each successive level they achieve, they add another element, until at the fifth level they have built the whole sigil. Here, the order of the elements matters, as well as how the sigil grows step-by-step over the course of study.

Now, what about replicating a sigil after it's been created? For the vast majority of shared magic sigils, I tell folks to start at the point to which they feel most drawn. The Sigil Fairy isn't going to come and bop you on the head if you don't draw it in the order I drew it. Heck, who's to say I even remember where I started drawing that sigil years after I created it? Still, there are certain sigils that do have an advised order. For example, check out the Bullseye Ballot Sigil on page 182, which includes directions on exactly how to draw the sigil. When a sigil has an order in which it should be drawn (at least for my creations), I'm telling the end user that there's a specific energy pattern they should follow to help promote the success of the sigil. Because as they are drawing the sigil, they are also connecting to the story of the sigil and its individual parts, which each have a layer of meaning.

On a related note, some folks ask how much their copy of a sigil needs to look like the original. I expect that if you're freehand drawing a shared magic sigil, there's going to be a bit of you in it. I can't even perfectly replicate my own sigils without tracing them, but I can get pretty close by paying attention. The natural slant of how I draw, the speed at which I'm copying, the surface I'm drawing on, and the materials I'm drawing with will all change the look of the sigil. But we're not shooting for

---

20. Laura Tempest Zakroff, "A Witch's Sevenfold Waning Moon Spell for Magical Resistance," *A Modern Traditional Witch* (blog), *Patheos*, June 6, 2020, https://www.patheos.com/blogs/tempest/2020/06/a-witchs-sevenfold-waning-moon -spell-for-magical-resistance.html.

clones here. If ten people all draw the same sigil, each one might be a little different in execution, but visually you'll be able to tell without a doubt that they're all the same sigil.

Symmetry, Asymmetry = Balanced Design

Many of my sigils appear to be symmetrical in design. From a technical perspective, that means that the included elements are equal and face each other around a defined axis. Symmetry as a larger concept is more about the balance of how something looks and feels than a perfectly mirrored image. When something is symmetrical, the viewer gets a sense of satisfaction or pleasure from the configuration. Visual balance isn't always about having perfectly mirrored or bilateral symmetry, which can sometimes be too static-looking.

Let's look at a few ways you can achieve a balanced look. A pair of shapes might be placed diagonally from each other instead of mirrored. Elements that have the same visual weight but are different in nature could be placed in bilateral positions, giving a sense of balance. Even though it isn't true mirrored symmetry, the design feels balanced because of the similar size and placement.

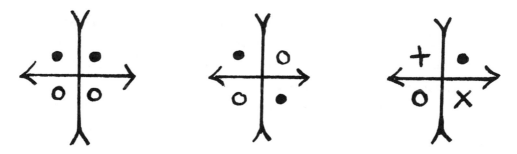

Examples of Symmetry: Mirrored, Diagonal, and Divergent Elements in Balance

What about asymmetry then? Most people confuse asymmetry with disorder, mess, or being unbalanced, but purposeful asymmetry *is* balanced by nature. When a designer refers to asymmetry as an applied concept, they're referring to a juxtaposition of different elements that yields the desired emotional or mental result. Accent walls, a statement necklace that stands out against traditional attire, a splash of pattern among solid tones—all are examples of working with asymmetry. These applications play with size, placement, and sometimes even the unexpected. Asymmetry creates visual interest, guiding the eye without creating obvious distress.

How you choose to compose and balance your sigil is largely determined by what you wish the sigil to accomplish. If the basis of your sigil is movement, then you're probably not going to want to make something that looks like it's immobile. Inversely, a sigil that is about creating foundation should feel like it's got a strong base. A protective sigil for a home might look like a fort and use a square as its dominant element, while a sigil for safe travels might have a circle that rolls with the person.

The 2021 Sigil for the Year (Symmetrical Design) and
the 2020 Sigil for the Year (Asymmetrical Design)

Another benefit of symmetry is that it can make the design easier to remember. Our brains tend to respond well to repetition and pattern-making. A simple design that has a limited number of elements in positions that are easy to recall makes the sigil easier to transmit to others. A sigil that has a lot of different elements and no obvious sense of organization to it tends to be harder for the brain to visually grasp onto and replicate. Now, if your goal is to create a highly complicated sigil that you don't wish to apply again in any other way, then the confusion created by the complexity might be seen as a perk. You might want to go this route if the purpose of the sigil is to help you forget something painful (as part of a healing process) or to hide something from others.

TECH TIP: HOW TO CREATE MORE "PERFECT" SIGILS EASILY

If I want a sigil to be symmetrically mirrored and equal, I accomplish this effect by drawing the sigil how I generally want it to look. From there, I scan in the art or take a high-resolution photo of it with my phone and send it to my computer. Next, I use an image-manipulation program such as Adobe Photoshop to isolate the parts I want to mirror.[21] I copy, paste, and flip them, adjusting as necessary. I find that this approach saves me a lot of time, versus trying to produce a "perfect" drawing. It also allows me to preserve the hand-drawn feel of my work, rather than making it look computer-generated. There are likely phone apps that can accomplish similar results, but I like to use what I'm comfortable with. Plus, if I scan in the image at a very high resolution, it makes it easier to transfer the image to other media, like stickers and shirts.

Eliza Gauger, the creatrix behind the incredible online series and physical book *Problem Glyphs*, initially used a free open drawing program called Alchemy to create her works.[22] At the Seattle release party for her book, she talked about the program's "mirror draw" function, which is how she achieves symmetry in her sigils. Alchemy was designed to help the user focus

---

21. There are free design desktop programs such as GIMP, if you don't want to invest in something like Adobe Creative Suite or Corel Draw. If you're a student or teacher, you may have access to free or discounted software.
22. Alchemy, an open drawing project, can be accessed at http://al.chemy.org.

on the drawing experience and has several other unusual features that help push your creativity, such as the ability to use your voice to control the width of a line or a shape's form. You can also draw "blind," which turns off the display feature—something useful with automatic or trance exercises.

Unfortunately, Alchemy hasn't been supported for several years now, so it's considered to be abandonware, but the site is still worth a look for ideas and may work for some users. There is also a plethora of newer free or low-cost drawing programs for tablets, including Procreate and Adobe Fresco. You could implement some of Alchemy's creativity concepts fairly easily with these programs.

The Passenger by Eliza Gauger

I Have the Touch: Personal Space, Reduction, Repetition, and Connection

If the question I get the most about my sigils is about symmetry, the next one is "Do all the elements have to touch?" The simple answer is no.

If you look at the Power Sigil on page 162, you'll see that the crescent moon and dot elements are not connected to the larger image, but float just outside the star. But their floating position and exterior placement still have meaning that's integral to the design. The crescents are both guarding the dot "seeds" that represent the legacy we wish to protect and marking the passage of time. The seeds are cradled in the vulnerable parts of the star, their physical separation indicating that they are on their own course. These future-minded elements remind us that in saving even just one person, we work to save worlds. So the inclusion of these marks in the design and their proximity connects them in concept to the star and the greater message.

In the example of the healing sigil shown here, the variation on the left, with its open space between the elements, allows for a greater sense of flow and movement within the core of the design. That feeling is stifled somewhat when most of the elements are connected directly together, as seen in the variation on the right.

Whether elements touch or maintain personal space reflects their relationship in the sigil. Also, whether the mark is located in the interior or exterior of the design can communicate purpose and relation. I recommend thinking about these ideas rather than worrying about making everything touch (or not touch).

Ask yourself: What does it mean for something to be in direct contact with another element or separated from it? Is it connected to the energy and intent of the other mark, helping to build or amplify it? Or does it need to perform its own action in the sigil?

Variations in the Proximity of Elements in the Design of a Healing Sigil

Alongside the question about elements touching is "Do I need to represent in my sigil all the shapes I brainstormed, or can I reduce the number of them?" In the most common chaos magic sigil-making method, you eliminate duplicate letters. So if your statement includes the letter *R* three times, you reduce it to one. I tend to do this with symbols and marks, but to me it's more a practice of condensing and combining similar elements to clarify the message.

You could look at multiple duplicate marks much like gathering grains of sugar to make the whole cup you need for a cookie recipe. Sometimes you need to add ¾ cup when you mix the cookies, while the last ¼ cup gets sprinkled on top for texture.

For example, If I brainstormed *building community* and *protection*, and I felt they each could be represented by a circle, then I wouldn't have to draw two separate circles to include them. A single circle could represent both points. But I might also draw a smaller circle to represent the community core and create a secondary circle around the first one to emphasize protection.

Another way to combine elements is to look for what the symbols and marks have in common.

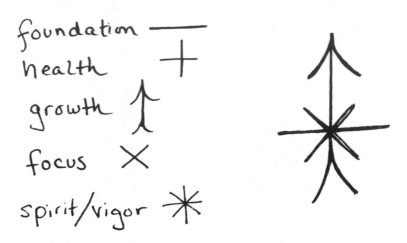

foundation ———
health +
growth ↑
focus ✕
spirit/vigor ✳

Consider Where Marks Can Merge

On the left in this example, we see the workboard with its brainstormed list of words and symbols. On the right, we see the sigil with all of these elements merged together. The horizontal and vertical lines can be intersected, which also forms the plus sign for health. This intersection might be the ideal place to place the X for focus, which in turn creates the asterisk. Where symbols and marks overlap or combine can add more layers of meaning to your sigil.

In the realm of touch and no-touch, we should also consider the concepts of positive and negative space. When an object is placed on the paper, it is existing in positive space. The undrawn space around it is the negative space. If we put two squares next to each other but not touching, the squares themselves are positive space, while the space between them is considered to be negative space. How far or how close the squares are to each other helps describe their relationship. The negative space in turn becomes a defined space as well, even though it includes no drawn elements. Rather, the space between the squares becomes visually implied or recognized as its own shape.

If the passage between the squares is wide, we might see it as a road or space that provides an opportunity for a range of movement. If the space is very narrow, the pathway may feel more channeled, like a cattle ramp—very defined and focused, with limited movement.

Space, connection, reduction, repetition, and positive and negative space might seem like a lot of ideas to hold in your head, but they're simply the names of concepts you likely already feel intuitively. Putting words to them can help give a little more form and sense to your internal sense of what is working—or why it's not. They help you narrate the story of your sigil as you design it.

Popular Symbols, Icons, and Letters

You'll see that I tend to lean toward using shapes and marks that are very simple, rather than pulling on popular symbols that tend to have a lot of information associated with them—like the peace sign or the dollar sign. This preference is strictly personal, which means I'm not going to tell you that you can't or shouldn't use those kinds of symbols in your work. But depending on what your sigil is, they may distract more than direct.

If I'm looking to draw wealth and prosperity, rather than drawing a dollar sign, I'm likely going to use a diamond shape. The diamond I use is a four-sided shape, and the number four represents stability, strength, and foundation. Diamonds themselves are highly durable as well as perceived as valuable culturally. Lastly, the diamond shape refers back to playing cards, which relate to the suits of the tarot's minor arcana. Diamonds equate to pentacles, discs, or coins; are earth-based; and generally deal with physical wealth, health, and work. This provides a huge amount of symbolism that goes beyond the dollar sign for me.

Similarly, if I want to bring the concept of peace into a sigil, there are multiple ways I could depict peace without referencing the more popular symbol that was designed in 1958 by Gerald Holtom as the logo for the British Campaign for Nuclear Disarmament. For the sigil I'm working on, I ask myself if peace means calm, unity, an end to fighting, open communication, etc. I might select a horizontal line, a circle, a series of wavy lines, or chevrons, depending on the interpretation.

As for letters, they can be very useful for representing people without using a whole name or trying to figure out what symbol a person should be, though someone's zodiac sign can definitely work in a pinch. Both letters and signs can be distracting design-wise, but at least they have a more precise association for how you're using them. I recommend using them sparingly though, and as a touchstone for a person or other kind of being if it makes the most sense to you. Letters (and most of the zodiac signs) can also be reduced to basic shapes or merged with other marks found in your sigil.

My suggestion is to dig deeper when you can, instead of defaulting to symbols and icons that contain a lot more meaning or recognition than you may be looking for. You don't need to have a literal visual translation of each item. Rather, remember to consider how the energy of a mark can relate to your brainstormed element.

Making the Ambiguous Concrete

Design is about problem-solving, and sometimes that problem starts long before you start drawing. One such instance is when you get stymied by what seems to be an ambiguous or even very simple goal that feels difficult to brainstorm.

A great example of this was brought up in one of my monthly Patreon "Sigil School" sessions.[23] The issue was that the person was looking for a new therapist, but felt stuck beyond "I need a new therapist" as the goal. My advice was to consider what factors make up the ideal therapist for them. Brainstormed elements could include things like this:

- Able to schedule an appointment soon
- Takes my insurance or has a sliding scale I can afford
- Good rapport
- Does virtual sessions and is on the public transport route near me

---

23. Once a month my Patreon supporters can join in an informal hour-long session with their sigil-related questions, problems, and ideas.

- Queer-friendly
- Understands issues affecting trans folks
- Grasps and understands polyamory dynamics
- Is an excellent listener
- Able to give helpful and insightful direction for my situation

With those considerations, what seemed like a very flat, simple goal is expanded into concrete details that are ideal for crafting a sigil. You can get a very real sense of what the goal you wish to achieve actually looks like.

Sometimes ambiguous, open-ended goals might seem easier, but remember: magic follows the path of least resistance. Find a balance between being specific enough and too specific. Otherwise you'll quickly find out that while your magic technically worked, the result was less than ideal.

Refine the Design: Avoiding the Kitchen Sink

When is a lot too much? Let's look at a few ways to avoid making an overloaded "kitchen sink" sigil that's more complicated than it needs to be at three of the key phases of the creation process.

At Step 1: Determine Your Goal

Remember that you want to be specific yet not too precise about your goal. If I've said it a thousand times, it's still not enough: magic follows the path of least resistance. If you select a goal that's too large and vague, it will be hard to narrow things down. "I want to be prosperous" is not very specific. How or in what ways do you want to be prosperous? Are you looking for a new job, for your business to expand, for your garden to be fertile and grow, to be financially comfortable at where you are in your life, to be very productive in your work or hobby? These are separate goals, with very different elements required for them to be successful. There's no reason why you can't create a sigil for each of them over time. But trying to smash them together into a very vague statement will take even longer, as there's not really a clear vision.

At Step 2: Brainstorm

I look at having six to eight brainstormed items as the sweet spot—not too few, not too many. That doesn't mean you're failing if you end up with as few as four or as many as twelve. It's simply a nice target to shoot for without making things too complex. When I create a Sigil for the Year on my Patreon, my patrons all contribute words or phrases they'd like to see for the year to come. That means I generally start with at least two to three dozen or more suggestions for things to include. So what I do is draft up the whole list of words and phrases and start putting them into related categories. Words and phrases like *networking, communication, interaction, voices being heard,* and *active listening* might all be condensed into one category, while *positive focus, hope for the future,* and *forward momentum* would be grouped into another. There's no reason why each item needs to have its own symbol if some of them feel very similar or the same to you.

At Step 3: Design the Sigil

If you've done a good job of being fairly specific about your goal and not overloading yourself with too many brainstormed elements, then you've already done a lot of the refining work necessary to avoid making your sigil more complex than it may need to be. But there's still a chance that could happen, and it's more likely to be the case when someone is first starting out, because they tend to be more concerned about making sure each element is distinct. But as we've seen earlier in this chapter, it's not necessary to have every mark and symbol clearly represented on its own. Reducing and combining related symbols or similar marks is one way to refine your design. Another way is to play with math. Do you really need 36 dots sprinkled around your sigil, or could you represent the number 36 by incorporating six asterisks that each have 6 points ($6 \times 6 = 36$)? If your sigil feels too busy to you, then it probably is. But if it seems like a lot yet still feels right to you and works for your needs, then roll with it. You can always revisit it later if you need to.

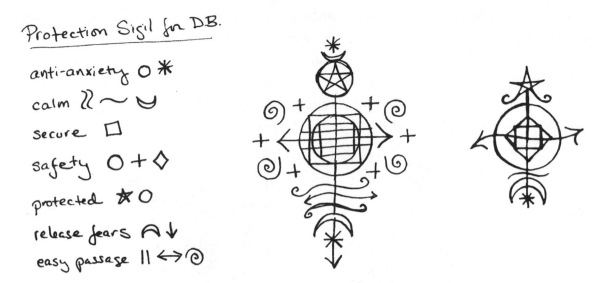

Protection Sigil for D.B.

anti-anxiety ○ ✳
calm ♫ ～ ∪
secure □
safety ○ + ◇
protected ✳ ○
release fears ∧ ↓
easy passage || ↔ ◎

A "Busy" Sigil versus a Simplified Sigil

Energetic Motion: Clarifying the Brainstorming Process

As we just discussed, too many elements in a sigil can make things confusing, while too few may not dig deep enough into the goal you wish to achieve. I find it helps to consider, "What does the solution look like? To consider my goal achieved, what factors would be included or key to that success?"

A key aspect to consider in brainstorming is the energetic motion of the intent. Think of it in terms of push or pull, block or free, slowing down or speeding up, open or close, listening/receiving or broadcasting/projecting, hiding or revealing, etc. One might classify a working as helping versus hexing or positive versus negative, but that lacks a lot of nuance and also ignores the fact that what is "good" and "bad" is very much in the eye of the beholder.

Let's consider the energetic motion involved in blessing a home. The goal is to protect the building, the land, and its inhabitants, shielding them from harm/ill intent and keeping them safe. However, we do want good fortune and good health to be able to enter, and for welcomed friends, family, and visitors to be able to find the house. So we're not setting up a blockade or trying to hide the home completely. We're looking for a feeling of protection from unwanted things while having some permeability for what we wish to draw to the home.

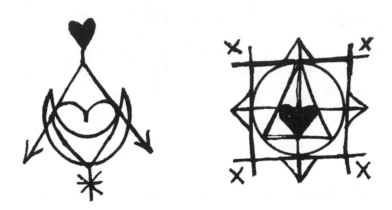

Home Blessing Sigils: A More Successful, Permeable Design
versus a Less Successful, Blockaded Design

It's also entirely possible that what you're looking to achieve is twofold (or more), requiring multiple sibling sigils to tackle specific parts of the job. This approach is a good option to consider if you find you have way too many brainstormed elements, and they seem to be working in opposition to one another or have very different focuses. For example, you might create one sigil to stop an abuser and bring them to justice, and a separate sigil to help aid and heal those affected by the abuser's actions. As justice would definitely aid in the healing process, it can be a connecting element between the two sigils or be a prominent design feature in both, *visually relating both sigils.*

Sibling Sigils

Separating out ideas into multiple but related sigils also can help inspire different ritual activities. As with our example sigil above, you might start off with a protection ritual with the first sigil, followed by a justice ritual to coincide with a court hearing using both sigils, and lastly follow up with a healing working with just the second sigil. We'll explore more about crafting rituals with sigils in the next chapter.

A Solution—One of Many

The sigil that you design for your working is *a* solution, and the one that feels the most on point at that moment. That doesn't mean that other solutions are invalid. It also doesn't mean you have to go exhausting yourself creating a multitude of designs after you've already decided that this one is good. In my workshops where we craft a sigil together as a class, there are always at least a few folks who are already exploring the technique and come up with their own solution to what we're discussing. Some of those results look very much like what we collectively end up with, while others are completely different. Those different ones aren't wrong, but rather are influenced by the individual creator problem-solving for themselves. This method is an intuitive process based on your personal experience, so it should be expected that if you give twenty people working separately the same goal and brainstormed elements, some of those sigils will look startlingly alike and others will be unique. Where it matters is if you're creating a shared magic sigil for a multitude of people to use, in which case you'll want to decide on a single design for maximum clarity.

You Will Not Void the Warranty: Revisiting Sigils

Let's say you create a sigil and then six months or a couple of years down the line you'd like to modify it to better attune with your goals. Should you create a whole new sigil or just work with the existing one? If you are basically just building upon what's already been established by the sigil, then I don't see there being any issue with making some small changes. You're not going to void the warranty and make it stop working. However, if you have a whole new understanding of a situation, and what you'd like the outcome to be is very different, then you'll likely want to create a new sigil. Do you need to do anything special with the old one? No, but you may wish to do something anyway to satisfy the ritual part of your brain that wants a tidy ending. (See the end of chapter 4 for suggestions on how to retire a sigil.)

You will also not break the sigil if you feel pulled to alter it slightly just a day or so after creating it. Sometimes when you're working on a sigil, you reach a point where your brain goes, "Well, I guess this is good enough. Yeah, it's fine." But after a little rest and a fresh look, you realize that the sigil would look better if you shortened that line or connected those parts. Technically you're still in the design stage, so you can continue to refine a sigil until you feel satisfied with it.

The only time when altering a sigil slightly becomes a problem is if you post the sigil for others to use and then the next week decide that it's not right. Again, the world won't end and the goal will still be there, but your folks may not be too happy with you, especially if they carefully carved that sigil into fifty candles for a ritual (unless, of course, you don't tell them). So it's best to either stick with the original design for that working, or don't share it until you're 100 percent happy with the design result.

Draw Like the Wind: How to Art Better

Now that we've covered a slew of design considerations and technical aspects, we're going to wrap up this chapter with suggestions on how to improve your drawing skills.

Draw Every Day

I can't say or write it enough: drawing takes practice. If I had a dollar for every time I've heard someone say "I can't draw a straight line without a ruler" or "Even my stick people are terrible," I'd have a beach house in Costa Rica.[24] I've been taking art classes and drawing all my life, and my work still benefits from more practice. Even at the top art colleges in the world, everyone is going to start out their drawing class practicing making lines and marks. Get a small sketchbook and some pens (don't get just one or it will immediately go in search of others) and set aside five to fifteen minutes each day to make marks, doodle, trace things you like, and make gesture drawings (quick and loose line drawings that capture the form or movement) of pets, friends, and family.[25] Sign up for a life-drawing class or see if there's a free regular drawing meetup in your area. You might even meet some cool new friends!

Draw What You See

Folks with aphantasia have trouble visualizing something in advance. This makes them believe, "I won't be any good at drawing." You don't have to draw from scratch. Instead, look to the world around you for inspiration. If you get easily overwhelmed, then select one simple object to draw: a spoon, a jar, an apple, a flower, a statue—something three-dimensional with a defined shape. Set a timer (I suggest three to ten minutes, depending on your comfort level) and draw what you see. When the timer goes off, rotate or flip the object so you're looking at it from a different angle. Try doing this from at least three separate angles/positions. This exercise will build your observational skills while helping to build hand-eye coordination.

---

24. I should make a sigil for that.
25. If you're looking for additional drawing exercises, I recommend checking out Betty Edwards's book *The New Drawing on the Right Side of the Brain*, which is listed in the bibliography.

How to Get Good at Drawing Something

If you want to get good at drawing something, draw it. A *lot*. Also, study how other artists have drawn it. Play with drawing or painting in their style to get a sense of how they saw that subject and interpreted it. For example, if you want to be able to make botanical drawings, study and copy the old engravings that are in the classic herbal books, but also look at how a variety of artists interpret plants. Create a sunflower like Georgia O'Keeffe and Vincent Van Gogh. Draw from life. Don't worry if you think it sucks—stop judging and just keep going. You will see improvement if you keep at it.

Have No Fear

Begin anywhere. When practicing, avoid flipping to a fresh new page when your brain tells you that you messed up. Stop trying to bury the evidence, and instead keep working at it. It's okay to have multiple attempts on the same page. Draw right over them if you want. If you find yourself erasing everything you do, switch to a pen or marker. Eventually the nagging part of your brain will shut up and leave you be.

Be Kind to Your Body

It might not seem like it, but making art can be exceptionally hard on the body. Warm up your hands and arms before you get started by doing some shoulder circles, and stretch your neck gently by rotating your head softly. Open and close your fingers on both hands and do some wrist circles. Check your posture as you work. Watch your grip on your pen or brush, draw on slightly cushioned/receptive surfaces, and use tools that make drawing or painting easier, not harder.

Chapter 4
Ritual Application

The object of art is not to reproduce reality, but to create a reality of the same intensity.
—Alberto Giacometti

If you've taken my Sigil Witchery workshop, then you've heard me say, "There are four steps, but only three of them are absolutely necessary." Meaning, once you've completed step 3, nothing else is essentially required for the theoretical success of your sigil. Step 4 is "Apply and/or acknowledge your sigil." The condition of this step being "necessary" is something to ponder. It resides in the space between "Is some additional action or factor *needed* for this to work?" and "Do I *feel* application is an important part of the process for optimal success?" Why is step 4 helpful even if it's not technically necessary?

Step 4 sits in the realm of ritual. Ritual is how we connect to the world around us and find our place in it. We use ritual to create order, develop patterns and purpose, bring meaning, honor the cycles of life and death, mark the passing of time, mark transitions, enhance community, and seek to influence our sphere of existence. Marriage and initiation are rituals, but so is your daily morning routine. Ritual doesn't need to be "religious" in nature either, meaning connected to a certain deity or spirit, or organized religion. While ritual can be fancy and elaborate in nature, it can also be informal and practically invisible, mundane in appearance. Yet both can be very effective and powerful to accomplish what is deemed necessary. As embodied beings, we are drawn to *do the thing*. The action of ritual is satisfying to our minds, bodies, and spirits. When we combine ritual with artmaking, we can take our magical practice to the next level.

The Intersection of Ritual and Symbol

Whether we're looking at cave paintings in France, the muraled interior walls of Egyptian tombs, the lively Minoan frescoes, or the ceiling of the Sistine Chapel, art can be found sitting alongside ritual. We have long used art and symbol to bring power to our rituals, whether we're exploring the mysteries of existence, honoring death, celebrating life, or telling our myths.

While we may not know exactly what happened in those caves thousands of years ago that surrounded the making of art for our ancestors, we *can* look at what we've done since then in terms of art—and continue to do today. Symbols are used for identification and acknowledgment, the marking of territory and material ownership, as mnemonic devices, for communication of complex ideas, to entertain and tell stories, to establish permanence, to create patterns, to beautify, to separate, to instruct and guide, and so forth. In a ritual context, symbols of identification can become key parts of an initiatory experience, while symbols of unification tend to abound in marriage rites, and images of deities are often highlighted in devotional practices.

The kinds of rituals we do tend to fall into one or more of the following categories. To give you a better idea of where ritual and art meet, each category has some examples.

Contingent/Initiatory: centers on personal transition, need, or crisis
Examples: Degrees in certain traditions and paths often have specific symbols attached to each initiation that become part of the person's identity and practice until they reach the next level. Tattoos sometimes are used to acknowledge and mark transitions, such as the semicolon (;), which symbolizes affirmation and solidarity against suicide and other mental health issues.

Ancestral/Devotional: honors the deceased, deities, or spirits

Examples: Veves are symbols drawn in Vodoun practices to connect with the lwa. Prayer cards in Catholic masses often combine the name (and sometimes picture) of the deceased with an image or symbol of their favorite saint. A family coat of arms calls upon ancestry and connection.

Divinatory/Revelatory: for divining and revealing

Examples: Much of cartomancy (card divination) is deeply rooted in imagery, such as the tarot, Lenormand cards, and oracle decks. Runes, regardless of whether they are made of bone, stone, or wood, all rely on the drawn symbol. Tea leaves are read by deciphering what images they form.

Protective/Preventative: ensures the health and safety of people, land, animals, etc.

Examples: The Arabic nazar is an eye-shaped amulet worn to protect against the evil eye. The cimaruta ("sprig of rue"), Italian horn, mano cornuta, and mano figa are also worn for their apotropaic properties. A practice originating in Gullah belief, many porch ceilings and shutters in the American South are traditionally painted haint blue to ward a home against ghosts.

Seasonal/Cyclical: oriented to a moment in the lunar or solar cycle

Examples: Many of us honor the changing of the seasons by decorating our homes and altar spaces with imagery that is associated with that season. Wearing certain items of clothing (or choosing to be naked or purposefully unadorned) can represent attunement with the seasons or mark special occasions. We use symbols of the waxing, full, and waning moons to connect with the energy of the moon.

While you might not consider all of these examples "art," they all incorporate elements of design and carry meaning through image and appearance. There is both art and craft involved, as well as a visual communication of ideas.

But let's dig a little deeper into where art and ritual intersect. The artmaking process itself is an act of devotion, an exercise of focus, a gathering of intention. We create art to communicate, explore, and influence, to express what is often intangible and give it a face—many of the same reasons we do ritual.

When you draw a symbol, make a painting, or craft some other artful object, you are applying focus and dedicating your time. Time spent creating technically becomes part of a sacrifice, as do the materials involved. A sacrifice is considered to be an act of offering something of personal value to a deity, spirit, goal, or community. The deliberate destruction of a work after the ritual transmits yet another layer of sacrifice. The ritual sacrifice is both communication and a transaction that generally goes beyond the means of basic monetary commerce. When we make art, we are willingly submitting ourselves to the process, knowing it will take time, thought, and materials to achieve our result. Even if the end result isn't exactly what we planned, the process is often the most valuable part of the experience. Artmaking is never a "waste of time."

If the idea of ritual intimidates you, remember that not all ritual runs around screaming, "I am a ritual!"[26] So much of ritual develops organically, as you build up a pattern of doing. Over time you begin to realize that you have a favorite approach, a way you like to arrange your materials, places where you prefer to do certain tasks. Everyday ritual doesn't take away from the times when you may wish to craft something more elaborate. Daily ritual helps you build the muscles of experience so that when you choose to work toward a specific purpose that's more special or complicated, you're ready.

Imbuing Art with Intent

When I set forth to write this book and asked people what they were most curious about regarding magical art, the most common query was "How does one imbue art with intent?"

I think I would be quite the asshole if I replied with what my brain first conjured, which was "You just do."

---

26. See *Anatomy of a Witch* and *Weave the Liminal* for extensive information on crafting and performing ritual.

ARTS & THE CRAFT
ACACIA ORRIS

My studio is a sacred space. It is my chaotic microcosm in the macrocosm, with every element contained within it's very messy four walls. Land masses consisting of short towers of boxes and piles of rocks shift throughout the day as I move them to reach for a book or hammer hidden behind their tectonic might. In nearly every part of the room, metal sits in spools of varying sizes and degrees of entanglement. Fire occasionally erupts from the tip of a torch to render that metal into something yielding and flowing. Water swirls in my small quench or forms into dark lakes when a forgotten drink falls to the floor. It changes into steam and clouds at the pickle pot, mingling with incense smoke that swirls off the altar that sits opposite my workbench. The studio tends to be an overwhelming place for outsiders, full of trip hazards and the occasional cat.

The Arkenstone by Acacia Orris

Despite that chaos, when the studio door closes and I sit at my bench, I often feel a calm wash over me. It's as though those swirling elemental forces around me stop and hold their breath, waiting for me to direct them so that together we can create something new. I get to be the Magician of my microcosm, my place of work where I do "The Work."

Find out more about Acacia at www.Lapidify.net.

But, you know, I don't think my brain's answer was all that wrong. More about that in a moment.

Now, I think I would also be quite the asshole if I told you that you must perform elaborate rituals with precise words and dances and not deviate from your task until the art is complete.

That would be an insult to all of the snacks I have eaten, tea I have drunk, podcasts I have listened to, and cats I have petted while making art for deities, spirits, and spells. Not to mention the more than occasional social media breaks I've taken to check in on the world.

None of those things have impacted the end result negatively. That painting of Hekate that you love wouldn't become any less magical if I told you that I took a break to cook mozzarella sticks while working on it. Who's to say that wasn't part of her plan, anyway?

I think a lot of folks have a tendency to believe there's some secret ingredient beyond just doing the thing. In the occult world especially, we think there has to be some magic words, some gestures, some sort of divine, mystical process involved! But the secret is simply in the doing of the thing: the time spent focusing and creating. Essentially what is needed is to build up a practice that instills confidence and creativity in what you are doing.

But please don't take my talk of cheesy goodness as disregard for more poetic ritual or practical preparation. In fact, I believe it's in the latter that intention is set and the doors open for the work to become imbued with our goal.

ARTS & THE CRAFT
KJERSTI FARET

It's not so much that the end product of the "piece of art" is magical, but the process to create it is. Art is the language of self-exploration, and I work a lot with symbols to navigate situations, emotions, and questions. Once the piece is done (not that a piece ever really feels done; it's more like it's time to abandon it), it has served its purpose for me. A lot of my personal work is hidden in my closet and is not actually out for view. Not that I'm against showing it—I would love to have a gallery show to display everything—but for me personally, the purpose is the journey.

I think of creating art as my form of spellcraft. I'm beginning with this intangible idea or intention and birthing it into the world. The process of creation sets it out into the universe. Sometimes there is a ritual involved to get myself into the right mindset. Usually I have to put on specific music playlists to get there. The mediums I use are based on what atmosphere or vibe I'm trying to achieve. Sometimes it's ink, paper cut, gouache, embroidery, graphite, digital, or a mix of various ones.

This way of working came naturally to me. Like most artists, I've been crafting and drawing all my life. It's been a lifelong journey just to figure out how I like to work, and the process just evolved into this. I didn't quite realize what I was doing at first; it was very intuitive. Being conscious of it has given me more control, but I am still kind of letting myself be guided by a greater purpose or something. It's a sweet spot between intentionality and being open to possibility.

But of course not all art I create is this sacred work. I make art for my job, and while I enjoy that work as well, it's not the purpose of my life to create products. But drawing for my job all the time does give me lots of practice to perfect my skills for when I have time to do personal art.

Creating is also my form of self-care. There is no hiding from the shadows when I do this. If anything, I embrace them. I acknowledge the uncomfortable feelings like grief or depression and let them be seen through my marks on the paper. When I give them attention, they are satisfied, like a cat begging for a treat. Art is the treat—for me and the cat. Then we can curl up together in peace.

Find Kjersti at CatCoven.com and @cat_coven on Instagram.

Alchemy by Kjersti Faret

This is generally how I make art:

1. I get an idea or vision, or I am given a goal by a client.
2. I research the elements of that idea, vision, or goal. This could be reading or listening to mythology concerning a certain deity, researching historical/reference images, and making a rough list of things I think the work should have.
3. I do a rough sketch or several, working out the composition, how to incorporate key elements that will help visually transmit the idea.
4. I select my materials, preparing the surface medium and gathering paints, brushes, or drawing materials. I clear my workspace/studio and set up my materials and references.
5. When I feel ready, I sit down and make the art. While something small like a sigil can be finished in a relatively short amount of time, a painting will likely take several days or longer before it's near completion. I then reach the "stare at" phase, which means I periodically look at the work in different kinds of light from various angles, and make small adjustments as need.
6. I scan in the art, varnish it (if needed), and sign the work.

I know, it doesn't sound deeply mystical. Yet this ritual is profoundly effective and is the result of decades of developing my artistic and magical practice. From beginning to end, my brain is focused on the process. My body naturally enters a kind of trance state when I start drawing or painting, and my studio is essentially my temple. What I'm doing with art is not very different from gathering oils, herbs, candles, and other ingredients for a spell and putting them all together.

Now, there are times when I feel inclined to do a little something extra. I may light a candle or anoint myself with an oil to help focus. If I'm doing a commission for someone that involves a deity I don't tend to work with, I may set up a small altar with items associated with that deity.

So truly it comes down to figuring out what helps *you* focus. If you feel your process will be aided by adding some extra ritual elements, then by all means do it! Here are some suggestions of ways you can do that:

- Cast a circle or set up a temporary temple space if you're working someplace that isn't dedicated just to magic or making work. Not only does this casting separate and define the space for you, but it can also be used to reduce possible distractions and interference.
- Consecrate or bless your art materials like you would any other magical tool.
- Create an atmosphere that is conducive to making magical art—consider lighting, music, incense, etc.
- Build a mini altar that aligns with your goal. If it's a spell, you could gather herbs, stones, or a certain color of candles. If it's a deity or spirit, you could have an image of them, plus an offering plate or other items associated with them.
- Consider where you physically create art an actual altar. Essentially, an altar is where action and communication happen. What would help turn your table, desk, or floor into an altar?

Lastly, remember that if you define what your purpose or goal is as you begin, then that sets the framework for everything you do. Even if you take breaks, the purpose is still a steady target. It is possible that what you imagined the art would look like will change as you go, but that is not a sign of deviating from your intention. Rather, see it as clarifying your vision as you work.

In the next section we will look at what can happen when we introduce coworkers of the spiritual kind to the process, how that can affect our purpose, and factors to consider when using sigils in ritual.

Art, Deities, and Spirits

There has long been a lot of conjecture about who or what is depicted in the figurative art of ancient cave paintings and petroglyphs. Are they meant to be us, spirits, deities, alien beings, shape-shifters, magical workers?

Why not all of these? We see the same kinds of art exploration around us today in our books, movies, plays, and art. We have a very long and fairly well-preserved global body of art that depicts not only deities but also amazing humans and mysterious creatures. We have always been imaginative and responded well to the visual form.

Some archaeologists speculate that early art must have been made to appease gods and spirits because our ancestors were overwhelmed by nature. I think that's more evidence of our own modern fears and disconnect from nature than a reflection of our ancestors' fears or religious beliefs. Long after we moved out of caves and into villages and cities, we continued to revel in making divine and mythical art. When we look at the history of art, we see that we have been constantly creating and recreating the gods in relation to our own image, plus imagining something just beyond that. Through art, we are communicating with the divine as much as we are discovering ourselves.

Let's examine some practical ways we can explore the divine and spirit worlds through art.

Working with Deities and Spirits

The visual art that I create to commune with deities and spirits tends to fall into two main categories: figurative/iconic and sigil/symbol. These two groups could also be separated into public and personal, respectively.

Figurative/iconic work is art that is either 2-D (paintings, drawings, prints) or 3-D (sculpture, costuming, jewelry) and that tends to give a face and/or body to the deity or spirit. There are almost always eyes that gaze out to connect with the viewer, which I feel is an important factor. The process of creating the art is private, but the end result is almost always very public,[27] as folks can purchase my

---

27. The end result is very public unless the art was created for a client or group who wish to use it exclusively.

original work and prints in a variety of formats. It is displayed in galleries, printed in magazines, and shared online.

The sigil/symbol work is generally a simplified line drawing that connects to or communicates with a particular deity or spirit. It is drawn in devotion to or in working acknowledgment of that being. Drawing the sigil during ritual can act as a temporary sanctioned gateway, depending on the tradition and rite. Another way to look at these kinds of sigils is that they are a door, and the dedicated practitioner acts as a specialized key when utilizing the sigil. That doesn't mean the door is always open, just like the door to your house isn't always open or unlocked just because you have a key to it. There needs to be intent, permission, and action in the application to access that door. Even in a static or inactive state, the sigil acts as a reminder of the relationship, which has a certain power of its own.

These kinds of sigils are usually created privately and are meant for personal work. There are sigils and symbols that appear in my figurative works, but those are meant to help others connect with the work/deity rather than utilize my own personal system. Basically, a deity or spirit sigil is a bit like having a private, unlisted phone number that only you know.

As a magical practitioner, you have the option of working with existing figurative/iconic art or creating your own. Making the art yourself definitely adds another layer of connection, since there's the whole creation process involved, but working with existing art isn't necessarily a lesser act. The end result of figurative/iconic work is a type of magic unto itself. It not only is a by-product of the creation process but takes on a life of its own as something others can relate too as well, without having been directly involved in the creation.

For instance, I love statues and I will gladly buy them if the image resonates with me. I *could* sculpt them myself, but I rarely have the time and access to the right materials to produce what I'd like to see. So when I come across a statue that depicts a deity as I perceive them, if it's in my budget, it's likely coming home with me. Purchasing artwork that has already been created isn't necessarily passive either. When we decorate a sculpture, set art in a picture frame, or place a candle or flowers before the icon, we are engaging with the art. These are all acts of devotion and communication.

ARTS & THE CRAFT
MATTHEW VENUS

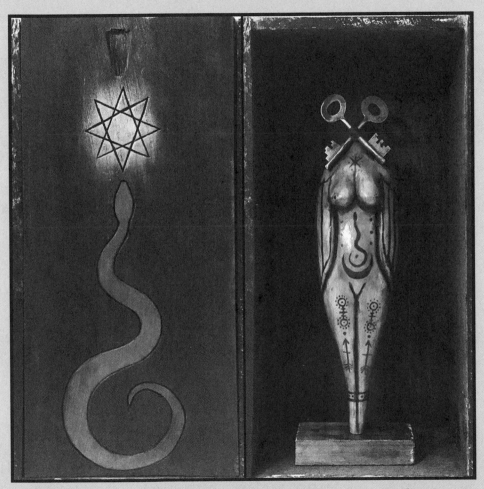

Spirit of Place Effigy Created in Residence at the Star & Snake by Matthew Venus

My approach to magic, spirituality, and the world is that of an animist, meaning that I believe all things can be said to possess a spirit and spiritual virtues which are reflective of their nature and history. This applies not only to natural objects and phenomena but also to those things crafted by our hands, to art. Many of the pieces I create are objects that are intended to be ensouled, or what we might call spirit vessels. Essentially they are intended to function as an earthly body for incorporeal beings. And for me this type of work inherently rests directly at the intersection of art and magic.

I usually approach such spirit vessels in one of two ways. The first falls more into the category of what might be considered spirit construction, wherein the materials and design of the piece become a part of the process of creating or revealing the spirit that will inhabit it. I am essentially bringing together various botanical, animal, mineral, or human-made materials, along with symbolic and aesthetic elements, to create a bit of a chimera from disparate elements. In these cases it is sometimes difficult to discern whether through the act of creation the spirit itself is being constructed, or if perhaps instead the inspiration (a term whose etymology is worth considering here) for the piece is actually a form of communion and co-conjuration between a previously undefined spirit and the crafter.

In the second approach, I am crafting spirit vessels/houses for previously known and established spirits/deities. These creations often serve as devotional objects, focal points of ritual, and icons, as well as spirit vessels. And in this approach it's a bit more focused on bringing elements together that are in alignment with and pleasing to the spirit or deity in question in order to create a sympathy between the spirit and this devotional anchor in the material realm.

Through the art of crafting spirit vessels, or, arguably, creating art in general, we are engaging in a couple incredibly meaningful and magical processes. First, we are doing for incorporeal beings what they cannot easily do for themselves: We are giving them body, form, and physicality. We are conjuring spirit into matter through an act that is simultaneously one of offering, devotion, and birthing. Through this process we are able to take the hand of the unseen and unmanifest, walk it across the veil, and create a point of access, a body for it to dwell within in the physical realm.

An Effigy Created to Serve as a Spirit House by Matthew Venus

Second, such an act is one that is ultimately the conversation between spirit and matter, and when we as artists stand as access points for the process, we are aligning with a form of "godhood" or divinity. We are the maker, the crafter, the artisan, the conjurer, the sorcerer, the Creator. And in the process of crafting "bodies" of matter—which are meant to be inhabited by spirit—we are like so many of the gods of old who were said to have sculpted humans from clay and breathed life into (inspirited) them. By aligning with our creativity and engaging in the creative process, communing with what inspires, we are connecting with our divine nature while also participating in something fairly unique to the human experience—namely, to desire to create the world in our own image.

Find out more about Matthew at SpiritusArcanum.com and @Spiritus_Arcanum on Instagram.

I'm less likely to personally use a public sigil or symbol unless it's part of a tradition of which I am a part (which usually means it's not public anyway). I often see folks online struggling to find "the oldest" or "the best" symbol/sigil to work with this deity or that spirit. When I check out the thread, I see that so-called "ancient" sigil was something that was first made up and published in a grimoire in 1998.[28] As I'm obviously advocating for creating your own sigils here, I'm not saying there's anything wrong with that sigil from 1998. People just seem to think that older is better, and are not always forthright about how it was made or what it means. However, if a symbol has been consistently found to be associated with a deity for centuries (with the archaeological evidence to prove it), then it may be a good place to start.

So how do you know when it's a good idea to create your own deity or spirit art? For figurative art, if you can't find work that fits your idea of the deity (either in existence or within your budget), then definitely give artmaking a try. You can also use the process as a way to become closer to that deity or spirit and expand your knowledge of them. If you look through my portfolio, you'll see there are several deities of whom I have made numerous paintings over the years. Each painting is an exploration of another aspect of our relationship.

---

28. Sorry, y'all—1998 may indeed be the last decade of the previous century, but ancient history it is not.

Guidelines for Making Figurative/Iconic Deity and Spirit Art

- *Do your research, part 1:* Read the myths and folklore associated with that being. Look to as many sources as you can. Make note of what resonates strongly with you. Visit the anthropology section before you visit the new age/magical section to see what's in the historical record. There *are* better deity books recently published by the occult/magical community, but there's a lot of misinformation and shoddy research out there too. Accounts of UPGs (Unverified Personal Gnosis) can absolutely tap into the essence of a deity or spirit, but sometimes they are presented as historical truth versus one person's spiritual experience.
- *Do your research, part 2:* Look at the art that's already been inspired by that deity or spirit. Google image search is your friend here. Pay attention to body language, gestures, symbols, and settings—especially when they show up repeatedly in both paintings and sculptures over the course of centuries.
- Once you've completed your research and gathered your materials, decide whether you'd like to set up an altar as part of your process.
- Be prepared to have a conversation with the deity or spirit and be open to new information.

That last point is key to working with deities and spirits, and I can't emphasize enough how important it is to listen in the process of artmaking. For me, there is a space between what *my* idea of the deity/spirit is and *their* idea of how they wish to be presented. In my witchcraft practice, I have a vast and extensive working relationship with many deities. Very few of those relationships are what I would consider devotional, even though the art I am making will be used as devotional art by others. Much like hiring a photographer to shoot a professional headshot, my job as a witch artist typically is to create a portrait of that divine entity to put out into the world. So while it helps to have done my research and sketches, I have to leave room for input from the entity. I find it fascinating that in these sessions I often will learn things that I somehow didn't come across in my initial research but do end up finding in the historical record later on. If I held fast to my initial image/idea and didn't listen as I worked, I would miss out on learning more as well as creating a more effective image.

You might be wondering, "How can I tell if a deity or spirit is talking to me?" I think it's different for everyone, but I doubt the majority of experiences involve physically seeing and hearing them. The best way I can describe the experience is that I'm hearing words or seeing new images in my mind, but it's not my own consciousness. I may also encounter feelings that are also not mine. If something is working out well, there may be a sense of excitement and the art forms very quickly. If I'm off track, there's a pull or a drag, even if the work looks good to me. The art will basically fight me until I listen and adjust.

Thoughts on Crafting Sigils for Deities and Spirits

- Much of the practice described in this book is very witch-based in its approach. This means that I'm not talking about commanding deities or spirits with sigils but rather about using sigils to communicate/work with them on a peer or acquaintance level. Another way to say this is "power *with*" versus "power *over*."
- If you're looking to create a personal sigil to relate with a deity or spirit, you should have already established or be in the process of establishing a relationship with them. This is not first date/blind date material.
- Consider what you are both looking for from this relationship and why this sigil would be useful.
- Do create an altar as part of your working space. Share a little drink or meal with them as you set down to work. Add incense, candles, music—whatever feels right.
- Have a sturdy, blank drawing surface (like a sketch pad) and a drawing implement that's comfortable, reliable, and not easily smudged. A drawing marker, ballpoint pen, or 6B pencil are all good choices.
- Sit in a position that makes it easy to draw, and keep your drawing instrument in contact with your surface.

- Focus on the deity or spirit and state your intention. It can be as simple as "I would like to create a sigil to connect better with you. Please join me in this process."
- From here, depending on how you visualize (internally or externally), you may start to see images in your mind's eye, or you can gaze upon the blank surface of the paper and start to draw what you feel or see there.
- Allow yourself time to receive, draw, and play with what shows up. You might not get a whole sigil design from the session immediately. More may come to you in a dream later on or be apparent to you when you sit down to finalize the sigil.
- Finalize the sigil and try it out. You might draw it on a candle, anoint it on your body with oil, etch it onto a piece of jewelry, or make it into a permanent work of art that is situated on your altar. If you do the latter, you could cover the panel with a piece of fabric when you're not working at your altar.

The sigil may morph over time depending on your relationship with the entity and new information you might learn. If you eventually stop working with that deity, you can put the sigil to rest ritually.

Working with Land/Nature Spirits

While you could make figurative or sigilic art to connect with the genius loci (protective spirit of a place) or a nature spirit, I find that a more free-form, location-oriented approach is appreciated by the spirit. When I work with spirits of place, my art tends to be more focused on natural patterns than specific drawings. I may use groupings of leaves, sticks, natural poppets, and gifts of food, water, and native seeds to create site-specific installation art offerings. I am mindful not to disturb the natural habitat or leave offerings that could harm or disrupt the environment and resident animals.

For example, I wouldn't use salt in my art offerings unless it's already part of the landscape, such as salt residue by an ocean or salt flats in a desert. Nor would I leave anything synthetic, but only things that will biodegrade naturally without hurting plants and wildlife.

There are a few instances, though, when creating a sigil for working with these kinds of spirits is helpful. I might seek the assistance of land spirits to craft a sigil designed to protect an area from development, or reach out to the resident spirits of my home to make a sigil to guard our house and surrounding area. I would invite that spirit to work with me after introducing myself and leaving an appropriate offering. In more urban areas, another excellent option is service work rather than leaving an offering. Cleaning up trash and debris does not go unnoticed and is often appreciated by the local spirits.

Land Spirit Offering

Art and Ancestors

Can you use art to connect with your ancestors? Absolutely. Would I create a sigil to do that? Depends on the ancestor. If I wish to connect with one of my grandparents, I find it's easier to go to either a photo of them or an object that I associate with them, such as a piece of jewelry they wore regularly. The latter contains a familiar essence that often holds multiple memories, which makes for a strong bond. A photograph, on the other hand, contains their visual likeness, which hits another part of my memory recognition. It might not seem like art, but photography technically means "drawing with light."

You might know someone who has passed and had a certain symbol associated with them. It might have been a tattoo they got, or a cultural or professional rank, or something they simply resonated with that merged with their identity.

If I don't have any photos, objects, or even stories of a particular ancestor, I may consider doing a painting or crafting a sigil. It's like raising an antenna to broadcast further out. Follow the same process as working with deities and spirits to create your sigil.

Word Up: Ritual Doing

One expression that gets bantered around the internet is "Words have meaning." I think it's more accurate to say "Words have meanings." Much like how marks and symbols can have a variety of meanings, word context and usage can vary greatly, depending on who you're taking to, where and when, or what supernatural fantasy TV shows they've seen. *Charge* and *activate* are two words that cause a lot of confusion, so here's how I view them in a ritual context.

Charge

To *charge* something in magic typically has two main meanings or applications:

1. To energetically bolster something, much like you would charge a battery.
2. To give a creation a purpose, assigning it a task to do, such as "I charge you with the purpose of healing X."

I often see *charge* applied as something you do *after* a sigil is created (in other methods). For the Sigil Witchery approach, you're technically doing both *as* you are creating the sigil. You start with defining the purpose of the sigil in step 1. In steps 2 and 3, you are focusing your attention on what is going into the sigil and giving it power as you draw it. Again, you can call it a day after step 3, because the work has begun. Step 4 tends to be more about aiding your body and brain in acknowledging the sigil out in the world than specifically charging it, but there's clearly some nuance to be considered. Every time you redraw the sigil, you are refreshing or renewing it. But you're just continuing the process that started at the time of the creation of the sigil.

Activate

Activate tends to be used almost as much as *charge* when it comes to sigils, and usually again at the end of the process, very much like asking, "So where's the start button on this thing?"

Besides the fact that *activate* is not a term I use in my process, I can't help but think of the act of cooking or baking when I hear this word. At what point are you actually *doing* the thing? Take, for instance, the process of making cookies. Is it when you decide to make a certain recipe, when you pull out the ingredients, when you mix them together, when you add heat to them, when you let them rest, or when you eat the cookies? Or is it when your taste buds say, "That's a damn good cookie"? The whole process brings the cookie into being. And even the raw cookie dough is freaking tasty.

It's not one step that makes the thing; it's the entire process. And the process will vary from person to person, recipe to recipe, and so forth.

Take, for instance, candle magic. Some people go all out carving candles, making them from scratch, choosing specific ingredients and colors, anointing the candles with oils, etc., while other people just burn whatever they have on hand. Both methods work. Then there's the argument about how to properly extinguish a candle. Some people insist that the candle should be snuffed out with a candle snuffer or your fingers, and they often say that to blow the candle out is disrespectful. Others believe that by blowing the candle out, you're applying will or intent and fusing all the elements together in one moment (air and water in your breath, fire as the flame, and earth as the materials burning, all united by spirit), so they see snuffing out a candle to be stifling. Then there are practical concerns about spilling wax and spreading smoke.

None of these methods are right or wrong, or better. They're just different approaches leading to the same result. You can pretty much connect everything done in sympathetic magic and spell-craft to stimulating your brain. Color, touch, taste, sensation, activity, sight, associations—they all speak to the visual part of your brain.

As a young witchlet, I quickly discovered that even if I just started thinking about doing a spell, I would see almost immediate results. The change had already been set in motion, with no candles lit, no herbs gathered, and no oils used. I think most practitioners are familiar with this phenomenon but still feel better having a process or method to apply.

So with sigils and my method, the same idea is at play. The moment you sit down to think about what you'd like to work on, the spell has begun. As you work out the problem or goal in your head, you're basically writing computer code for your brain. In the design process, you organize the code into an order that makes sense, removes any unnecessary information, problem-solves, and creates a finished product. The moment your brain settles on a design that is pleasing to you, you've essentially hit the enter key. The programming is in motion. Anything you do after that moment simply furthers and/or refines the protocol you've established, like putting your sigil for good study habits on a cookie and eating it.

So what part of the process makes a magic cookie? All of them. The trick is not to get too caught up in the words or previously learned methods and to be open to new ways of doing things.

Trance Practices

When I get fully involved in the artmaking process, my brain and body automatically enter a trance-like state. There are many kinds of trances utilized in ritual, but we tend to picture the more dramatic and extreme ones, such as seemingly unconscious states where the body is utterly relaxed, ecstatic trance dances, and alternate states brought on by the use of psychedelics. For me, the type of trance I engage in when making art is a state of complete mental absorption or deep musing. I'm conscious, aware, and fully embodied, yet very much focused, calm, and comfortable in my task.

And all I had to do to get there was sit down to make art. I've done it enough times that my whole being recognizes what it needs to do. It just takes some practice to train your body to achieve that focused level of trance so you can remain on task yet still be receptive.

ARTS & THE CRAFT
DAVID MEJIA

Heracles vs. Achelous by David Mejia

For me, artmaking is delving in further beyond mere inspiration, digging down deep into the realm of the Self and being in a trancelike state to pull out the mythic and the creative. My best paintings have come from this deeper realm, and it even affects those who have seen them. I can always tell when I've tapped into something more because of how the Spirit of it moves and flows into the painting and won't let go. How do I get to that trance-like moment? With ritualized preparation of each item that I use to paint, sometimes by working in the public eye (as an introvert, being in public sometimes forces me further into my art), music ... Eventually the world drops away and it's just myself and the movement of painting.

Find out more about David at www.facebook.com/Mejia-Arts-122796911150958.

Automatic Drawing

There are slightly less focused yet similar states of trance that are also useful for artmaking. These allow you to explore and play. You don't always have to have a defined purpose with all the art that you make. You can just put pen or pencil to paper and see what comes. The drawing for my Mother Matrix sigil had no specific purpose or goal. I just needed to draw and let the image come as it wanted.

This approach is called automatic drawing. You can use automatic drawing techniques for divination, mediumship, and skill development:

- *Divination:* Sometimes the answers we're looking for can be revealed in what we draw or write. With this approach, think of a question, set a timer for three to five minutes (if you'd like), and allow yourself to simply start drawing. If you are feeling compelled, you can draw for longer if you wish.
- *Mediumship:* Automatic drawing can help you relax and open up mentally. Some people use this technique to help channel spirits or deities, with the belief that those

Mother Matrix Drawing (Pen and Ink Drawing by the Author, 2015)

beings can come through the entranced writer or drawer—sharing messages or images from other realms. Automatic writing was a popular technique especially at the height of the Spiritualist movement, but its roots are much older than that. Often all that's needed is to think of the person you'd like to contact and then let whatever comes to you flow out from your hand onto the paper.

- *Skill Development:* If you're uncomfortable with drawing, it's likely because you're judging the marks you make before they even get a chance to take form. You're placing too much importance on the end result and are mentally bypassing the process. Practicing automatic drawing can help you learn to shut off the critical part of your brain while becoming more familiar with the action of drawing itself.

There is the added benefit that automatic drawing doesn't require a lot of setup to get started. You just need to be in a relatively comfortable position (but not so much that you might fall asleep) and have a decent-sized surface to draw on (so *not* a sticky note, but an 11-by-14-inch newsprint pad would work well) and a trusty writing implement. You want to be able to have room for your hand and arm to move around without running off the paper. You also don't want a drawing tool that's going to run out of ink or go dull very quickly. A fresh (non-stinky) marker, ballpoint pen, or soft pencil will work nicely. You could also try this exercise with a tablet and digital pen using a basic drawing app.

Once you have gathered your materials and are comfortable, take three slow breaths. Hold the first breath for three seconds, the second for five seconds, and the third for eight seconds. This calms both your body and your mind. Gaze upon the blank surface of the paper and just let your hand move across it with your chosen tool. Don't strategize or try to decipher; simply follow the motion and let it come—whatever your hand wants to do. Allow yourself to draw for at least five full minutes before taking a break.

There are quite a few ways you can play around with this exercise:

- Try drawing with your non-dominant hand.
- Instead of watching the paper, close your eyes as you draw.
- Allow your mind to be fascinated with the feeling and motion of the mark being made versus how it looks.
- Try drawing in one continuous line, without lifting the tool.
- If you find you're over-focusing, use low lighting so it's harder to see what you're drawing.

I recommend setting aside fifteen to twenty minutes a week to explore this technique until you get the hang of it. It can also be a fun exercise to bring to a group ritual.

A Meditation to "Get into" a Sigil

If you're looking to integrate a sigil into your practice, whether it's one you made yourself or one you found, you should explore its energies through your mind and body. The best way to know a sigil is to draw it, and there are several ways you can do this. Each of the following methods will encourage a meditative, trancelike state:

- Practice drawing the sigil with a soft pencil or fluid pen over and over again.
- Repeatedly trace the sigil with your finger, either by printing it out on a piece of paper (large enough to accommodate your finger and any fine detail) or by pulling up an image of it on your phone, tablet, or computer screen.
- Use your whole body to draw the sigil.[29] By moving your arms, legs, hips, etc., you can build and express the shapes that make up the sigil and repeat them.

---

29. Visit my YouTube channel for several Witchual Workouts where I show you how to dance a sigil. Laura Tempest Zakroff YouTube channel, "Witchual Workouts" playlist, https://www.youtube.com/playlist?list=PL2TYo23upMtGqS-9RG4dtW8gHwdec3rAf.

- Draw the sigil on the ground with chalk, big enough to walk on, if you have the space and ability to do so. This approach makes the sigil into a kind of labyrinth path to follow.

The Measure of Materials

When it comes to making art, we humans have always begun with the materials most immediate and accessible to us: dirt, sand, rocks, charcoal, bone, wood, shells, blood, water. The ground beneath our feet, the stick brought down from the oak tree by a storm, the leftover charcoal from last night's fire—they might not seem valuable in modern terms, but using what's close by isn't lazy; it's practical.

Many materials have become embedded in tradition, acquiring significant lore and importance simply because they worked well and were readily available. Items such as salt, cornmeal, pigments, herbs, flowers, and seeds all represent sacrifices from what we would otherwise use for other means, as well as the initial investment of time spent collecting, growing, and/or processing them. Some of these items can go on to live other lives as well, eaten by birds, insects, and other animals.

There is a mentality that pushes the idea that you want to get the best, fanciest, most expensive materials, and if you can't, then it's not worth the effort. Not only is that a bunch of elitist bullshit, but it's simply not true. You don't need to spend a lot of money to make something worthwhile.

Of course, if part of the ritual involves having something that is long-lasting and durable, then you will want to choose your materials accordingly. If I want to make a sculpture for outside, I can't make it out of Play-Doh. It needs to be made of something that can withstand the elements. If I'm creating a painting for a temple, cardboard and chalk wouldn't be ideal. Rather, my materials need to be archival and durable, suitable for the task. But if I'm going to do some automatic drawing for an exercise, some newsprint paper and a piece of charcoal or a marker will do the trick.

If you're wishing to create something talismanic, there is also the magic of the materials to be considered. My friend and amazing esoteric printmaker Liv Rainey-Smith occasionally uses crushed semiprecious stones to hand-tint some of her alchemy-themed woodcuts.[30] There are ceramic artists who collect and process clay themselves to connect with the land. Some people prefer to make their own paper, infusing the fibers and pulp with specific herbs and crafting the sheets during specific phases of the moon or astrological hours. It's not that these materials are necessarily inherently expensive, but rather that they require time and thought to utilize them properly, making them special.

If you plan on doing a lot of art, it does often pay off to invest in quality materials when you can.[31] Some cheaply made materials are frustrating to work with and don't last very long. For example, with colored pencils, cheap ones have a lot more wax/filler than pigment, break easily, and are hard to sharpen. For a little more money, you can buy pencils that will last for years and provide a more satisfying drawing experience.[32] For the cost of three to four brushes whose bristles fall out every time you use them, you could have one or two brushes that are dependable and long-lasting. It pays to do a little research.

A good question to ask yourself is whether the materials work for what you need to accomplish. If the answer is yes, then you are fine. It's the artmaking process that's the most powerful part of the experience—and whether you spend a hundred dollars on materials or make do with what you have, the amount of money spent will not guarantee a significantly better or more effective sigil or work of art. A deity is not going to smite you because you opted for the student-grade watercolors that were in your budget versus the top-of-the-line professional-grade ones.[33]

---

30. See Liv's work at her Etsy shop, https://www.etsy.com/shop/Xylographilia.
31. In chapter 4 of *Sigil Witchery*, I cover choosing art materials. If you have a local store that's dedicated to art materials, it's very likely that artists work there and can make recommendations based on experience.
32. I still use the big box of Prismacolor pencils I bought in the late '90s. I just replenish the colors I use the most every few years.
33. If they do, I'd sincerely recommend finding another deity to work with, or tell them to get on increasing your budget if they want to make that kind of demand.

ARTS & THE CRAFT
POLLY LIND

I started to make magical art because I was looking for something that represented who I am and my magical practice and was created with sacred magical intent. I wanted something that was sacred, magical, and connected, and I wanted it to represent the land I live in. I live in New Zealand, where the seasons are opposite those in the Northern Hemisphere, and we cast our circles in the opposite direction, starting in the east and then tracking north, which is the same as what our sun does. Much of what was available at the time was seasonally and directionally reflective of the Northern Hemisphere and mass-produced, and it just didn't fit what I was after.

I use fabric to create all of my artwork. I call these pieces modern applique tapestry. Fabric just feels more sacred to me, in part because my mother and grandmother taught me to sew, and because fabric clothing and banners have been used as sacred adornments for altars, temples, sacred spaces, and people for probably as long as there has been fabric. I love the challenges of creating artwork using fabric and stitching, and it just feels right to create my artwork out of fabric. My scissors, pins, sewing

Elen of the Ways by Polly Lind

machines, fabrics, and cottons are my sacred tools, and my studio is a sacred space—my temple—where I create magical artwork.

I call the pieces that I create doorways. As I make each piece, I remember what I have learned from the research I have done and let the magic flow and connect to the deity or spirit image that I am creating, which in turn connects it to the piece I am working on. I leave it up to the individual who buys an original or a print to open the door. I cannot say how another person would go about opening their door, as it is such a personal thing. I imagine it can be done with ornate ritual or a simple prayer, or simply by knocking on the wall next to the hanging and inviting spirit or deity. Or if the person prefers, they can just have it as a lovely piece of artwork.

Find out more about Polly at www.PollyLind.com.

A Blessing for Art Materials

To help you get into a ritual mindset, you could do a short blessing of the materials you are about to work with. It's a great and simple way to prepare yourself to begin working and set an intention for the art.

Spirit, air, water, fire, and earth,
I bless these tools to guide my work.
With steady eye, hand, heart and mind,
Art to flow, inspiration find.

Ritual Art Projects

There are truly countless ideas for what you can do with magical art. Here are some ideas to get inspiration flowing:

- Make a painting, drawing, or sculpture of a deity or spirit to use as a focus for your altar.
- Incorporate spellcraft into your art. I love taking elements of traditional sympathetic magic spells and turning them into paintings and drawings. They can be small and simple or large and elaborate.
- Craft a ritual or a ceremonial mask or costume for specific rites.
- Create your own oracle or tarot deck.
- Make your own set of runes.
- Create talismanic jewelry.
- Craft ritual tools and vessels.
- Embellish an altar cloth or banner for your ritual space.
- Build a vision board to help you visualize your goals.
- Hand-bind and decorate a grimoire or book of shadows.
- Make your own personal sigil/identity/signature mark for your work.
- Create a pocket shrine or altar box for travel.
- Work together with others to craft a sigil for your coven or group that amplifies your focus.
- Create dolls, poppets, assemblage, and other sculptural magic pieces.
- Print magically themed fabric to use for altar cloths, tarot bags, or other ritual wear.
- Make your own spirit or Ouija board.

ARTS & THE CRAFT
KAMBRIEL

There has always been an innate element of witchery in my stitchery. Everything about the art of creation can be fundamentally based in magic as long as the intention is there to imbue a certain power, a certain hope, a certain transformation in what is being brought forth, from nascent intuitive thought to ultimate desired form. Clothing is ultimately a quite intimate and powerful art form since it is personally selected by the wearer to be worn directly against their body and thus carries with it an ability to strengthen the wearer's aura, to magnify elements of the essence of their character even before any words are ever spoken. It's an honor for me to be part of that process of enhancement, of reflection, and of transformation.

The energy and intention I create anything with is absolutely elemental to my work. I'll at times summon from darker places when creating for myself if the inspiration for a particular piece itself calls for it, but when creating for anyone else, I consider it paramount to imbue the work solely with positive enchantments. When such an elemental energy is imbued into the art one creates, when the entire work is embedded with conscious meditation, that piece will carry this original energy into the future. This makes it all the more vital for one to be quite mindful and purposeful of the energy pulled forth and stitched into any given piece throughout the process of bringing it to life, as those thoughts, those feelings throughout, will permeate the deepest formative thread of its being.

It's no accident that such focus has been placed on the raiments of the magical throughout time—the flowing robes, the shadowing hats, the tangled, silken, and woolen shawls. Personal garments are imbued with the spirit of the creator as well as the spirit of the wearer. Garments are wearable ghosts, both strengthened and haunted by their memories.

Photo of Kambriel by DividingMe

Find out more about Kambriel at www.Kambriel.com and @kambrieldesign on Twitter.

Sigil Applications

In *Sigil Witchery* I cover a wide variety of applications for sigils. For quick reference, I've included some of those ideas here, as well as some new ones to consider.

Outside the Body/For the Skin
- Use makeup or henna for temporary marks and tattoos for permanent ones, or anoint yourself with oil.
- Carve sigils into soap for washing the body.
- Paint or draw sigils/art on clothing or make jewelry (daily or special occasion) with them.
- Trace, walk, dance, or gesture the sigil.

Inside the Body (Food and Drink)
- Stir sigils into your beverage.
- Draw sigils on a tea bag or coffee filter.
- Cook sigils into food (sandwiches, cookies, pies, soups, etc.).
- Place art/sigils on a reusable bottle.

Inside the Home
- Draw sigils on doors and windows for protection.
- Place sigils on candles.
- Adorn altars with sigils.
- Draw sigils in the air with stick incense or a smoke wand to cleanse a space.

Outside the Home
- Place sticky notes with sigils or hidden sigils in the workplace.
- Place sigils on stones or markers around your property.
- Draw sigils with chalk in gathering spaces.
- Draw sigils on cars and other vehicles.

Any of these ritual art projects and sigil applications can be done in ways that are as simple or complex as you wish. It all depends on what you're looking to achieve from the experience. Before you do anything, though, ask yourself, "Does this sigil (or piece of art) make sense with this application?" If you do what's appropriate rather than just what's easiest, you'll likely be pleased with the results.

After the Art

Another big question that folks have about art and magic is "What do I do with the art after my goal has been achieved or the work has been finished?"

I have to admit this question was a bit of a surprise for me at first. As an artist, the general circumstances are the following: I make art, then I either keep it or sell it (or pass it along in some way). When I finish nearly every painting, my partner asks, "Do we get to keep this one?" Obviously if the work wasn't created as a commission for someone else (so it has a home), the options are to keep it or sell/share it. Sigils get shared (as they're largely meant to be distributed if they're community-oriented), but paintings take up significant space. If they didn't move on to a new home, we would be buried alive in art.

But I know that's not really what folks mean when they ask that question. They want to know what to do with the art after the task has been completed. Is it safe or smart to keep it around? Do you need to hold on to it, or can you let it go?

I think the answer largely depends on why the art was created and how it was intended to be used. Some art is designed to decay. You could look at a spellcraft piece of artwork like a vinyl record. You can put a record on anytime to have a listen and stow it away the rest of the time. With a work of art, you can pull it out for specific occasions and then return it to storage when you don't need it.

Some pieces have a sense of sacrifice built in—they are meant to be destroyed once the work has been completed. It could be that the magic is tied up in the making of the object; the process is what is devotional and the end result is meant to be destroyed. Other pieces act as a chrysalis—a vital container that acts as an incubator until the desired change has occurred—for example, a protection spell while someone is going through an ordeal, or a binding spell until someone has overcome a bad habit or behavior.

Other pieces of artwork are dearly loved and used but meet an untimely end. Perhaps that beautiful handmade offering bowl was accidentally dropped and it broke. Maybe your basement ritual room got flooded and your deity painting was ruined by water and mold, or moths ate your ritual mask. Art tends to be much more ephemeral than we think. It's no match for fires, hurricanes, tornadoes, and mold. All these things do happen, and sometimes there's no saving the art. This is heartbreaking and often leaves the practitioner wondering what to do with the sad remains.

For these situations, I often turn to the elements to ritualize the next step:

- *Water:* purifies or dissolves
- *Air:* inspires/spreads ideas or disperses
- *Fire:* transforms or eradicates
- *Earth:* roots or covers/submerges

If you want to ritually retire a sigil or other piece of magical art you've made, here are some ideas. Now, if you're keeping track of sigils in a grimoire or sketchbook, please note that you do not have to destroy your book or rip out the pages. It's good to keep a record of what you've done, including the purpose, date, and other important details. Retiring a sigil or other piece of artwork is more about the ritual process for our own satisfaction and sense of completion. You can create the sigil on paper or other material one more time (outside of your book) to use for the ritual, if you don't have something made already. The process of drawing it one last time with the application of the retiring ritual helps bring everything full cycle at once.

- *Dissipate it in air:* Draw the sigil with incense or an herbal smoke wand, ideally outside where the wind can take it away.
- *Release it by fire:* Draw the sigil on a piece of paper or a dried leaf and burn it in your cauldron. Spread the ashes or bury them.

- *Dissolve it in water:* If you're landlocked, draw the sigil with salt, honey, or something else that will easily dissolve in water. If you're near a body of water like a stream or ocean, draw the sigil in the sand/mud where it will be washed away.
- *Bury it in earth:* Draw the sigil on something compostable and bury it with love and appreciation. A nice added touch is to set seeds or a plant on top of it.

What makes retiring a sigil different from applying it at the beginning of the cycle is your intent and a sense of gratitude and appreciation for the work accomplished. As you engage in any of these processes, keep in mind that you're not destroying the work as much as acknowledging the change in relationship as you move on.

Truly, there are as many ways to interact with your sigils and magical works as there are stars in the sky. What matters most is that the ritual works for you and what you need to do in your practice.

A Gratitude Ritual or Blessing for Retiring a Magical Work

If you are storing a piece indefinitely but want to preserve it, you can make a ritual out of the process of wrapping it up and putting it away. It's best to store artwork using archival materials, such as acid-free materials and light-safe boxes. For sigils, you could keep a special folder or photo box to hold the drawings once you're done. For larger art pieces, you may wish to wrap them in fabric and stow them in a suitable container. When you're done wrapping up your work, you can draw a pentacle on the container (and/or consecrate it with the actual elements if you'd like) and say:

Within the elements I give you rest,
Acknowledging the magic you have blessed.

If the piece has been given a name, you could start by addressing it as such. For example:

To my Sigil of Place, within the elements …

I like to also add a simple "thank you" at the end.

A Ritual to Renew, Repurpose, or Renovate a Magical Work

Sometimes you'll find that you'd like to bring back a piece that you retired. You might need it again for the same purpose or need to modify it in some way for a related purpose. If it's something you never officially retired or put away but just stopped actively using for a while, then you can use this ritual as well if you'd like to rekindle the relationship. As you say the words, you can use the actual elements to bless the work, but be careful not to damage the piece by accident. If you're worried about damage from water, fire, smoke, or salt, then just use elemental symbols instead or place the work in the center of a circle of active elements (candle, bowl of water, salt, incense, etc.).

> *Welcome back, O being of art!*
> *Awake again, time to restart.*
> *With my words, I bless you with air,*
> *Water kissed and blessed by fire fair.*
> *Earthen mark drawn and spirit made—*
> *Begin again the magic laid!*

Now you can use the work as before or modify it to suit your needs.

Appetite for Creation

You have reached the end of Part 1: Create. Give yourself time to play, explore, and experiment with the ideas presented. Discover for yourself the feeling of trance-induced mark-making, uncover your own treasure trove of symbols hiding just below the surface, and build your confidence through practice. Find the rituals that make sense for your magical path and lean into them to increase your creativity and sense of wonder.

In Part II: Collaborate, you'll explore the possibilities of what can happen when you move past making art with yourself in mind and start to create collaboratively. From the power of art being out in public to crafting work communally as shared magic, you'll find a variety of important things to consider. You'll also find a collection of shared magic sigils to use if you'd like and to help guide and inspire you in your own future work.

Part 11

COLLABORATE

Chapter 5
Out in the World

I recognize the utility of imagery against hardship as a fundamental human experi-ence, and it can be said, the primary role of the public artist.

—Eliza Gauger, *Problem Glyphs*

In this chapter we'll look at sigils that are meant by their very nature to be out and about in the world, as well as how they work and what to consider when making and using them. Or, as I like to say, where the microcosm affects the macrocosm and has a party. Meaning creating an opportunity where the personal and the public can intersect, affecting the world magically.

It may seem strange or even heretical to some folks to create sigils that are designed for the public good, but art works for the personal experience as well as for communal benefits. The difference between a private sigil and a shared magic sigil is that the latter is created to have a larger focus and to be utilized by multiple individuals working for that common goal. Not only are there effective communal sigils, but there are also personal sigils that can be used in very public ways, such as sigils you might use to promote your business or protect a space. There's also the consideration of crafting sigils for others on a more individual scale. Collectively, all of these variations involve collaborating with others on some level, whether actively, subliminally, or otherwise. Choices made concerning a sigil's size and scale as well as its placement and exposure affect the audience and how they may be influenced by the work. Whether we work intentionally with or for others, we are forging a collaborative relationship between the art and the world around us.

Public Art Magic by Design

What does it mean when art enters the public space? How does it affect us? When most people hear or read the words *public art*, they generally think instantly of big murals on the sides of buildings and sculptures in parks. This kind of art beautifies public spaces and shows an obvious support for the arts, at least on the surface.

Many cities now have public art as part of their public planning mandate. For example, Seattle, Washington, one of the first cities in the United States to adopt a percent-for-art ordinance in 1973, mandates that 1 percent of eligible city capital improvement project funds be set aside for the commission, purchase, and installation of public artwork.[34] It often also works as a tax write-off for many big corporations and developers.

Sometimes public art isn't just a mandate or a write-off, but is part of the culture. In Providence, Rhode Island, the Avenue Concept (TAC) works with local businesses and organizations to fund and support the creation and installation of artwork in public spaces. As part of their mission statement, they believe that public art should invite engagement and interaction—not passive observation— and that art enlivens and improves cities, tells stories, and adds value to public spaces.[35] For example, in 2018 TAC helped create the six-story mural "Still Here" in cooperation with the Tomaquag Museum and the artist Gaia.[36] The image is of a contemporary young Indigenous woman holding a portrait of Princess Red Wing, a Narragansett/Pokanoket-Wampanoag elder, historian, folklorist, and curator, surrounded by native flora. According to TAC, the mural is meant to inspire as well as

34. "Public Art," City of Seattle, https://www.seattle.gov/arts/programs/public-art.

35. "About," The Avenue Concept, https://theavenueconcept.org/about.

36. "Still Here," The Avenue Concept, https://theavenueconcept.org/artworks/still-here.

celebrate the resilience of Rhode Island's Indigenous people. It certainly catches the eye and transforms the space in a powerful way.

Public art, especially in the form of large murals and big sculptures, is easy to point out. But we often overlook the art and design that is present all around us, interacting with us on a daily basis. It's so well woven into our modern lives that we tend not to notice it.

One of the most pervasive forms of influential public art is graphic design. The whole realm of graphic design is about capturing your attention, building brands, communicating ideas, and selling products or services. Or, as the American Institute of Graphic Arts (AIGA) in New York defines it, graphic design is "the art and practice of planning and projecting ideas and experiences with visual and textual content."[37] Graphic design is the manipulation of shapes, colors, textures, sizes, forms, and fonts to create connection, usually linked to an emotional and/or intellectual response. From an ad on the side of a bus or in your social media feed to websites, product packaging, and brand logos, they're all under the heading of graphic design.

Design isn't just limited to ads, websites, and book covers. Architects consider these elements when drawing buildings. Industrial designers utilize them in product design, from the dinner plates you eat on to the cellular phone you use. That public park you walk through was planned by landscape designers. They are all meant to interact with us, tell a story, invoke an emotional or mental response, even if it's more on the subconscious level.

Designers create visual content to communicate messages to a particular target market. Those messages utilize classic design principles such as balance, contrast, movement, proportion, rhythm, and emphasis, many of which are concepts we covered in chapter 3 for crafting more effective sigils. Similarly, in any graphic design project, there is a clearly defined goal and there are elements incorporated into the design to help bring about that goal. Then how the finished design is applied helps to reinforce those goals.

---

37. Juliette Cezzar, *The AIGA Guide to Careers in Graphic and Communication Design* (New York: Bloomsbury, 2018), 15.

So are logos, brands, and other kinds of symbols all types of sigils? It's a tricky question to answer, because once you start digging into symbols, you'll notice a lot of similarities to sigils. Much of what is often said to be required to work magic (will, intent, focus, and the manipulation of or influence over a person, place, or thing) is also part of the graphic design process. If you define a sigil as being "a symbol believed to have magical properties," then it really comes down to how you personally see the practice of magic and the application of belief.

The Art of Shared Magic

How does shared magic work? The premise is simple: big ideas require big help. The more folks, the more power/energy/attention can be directed toward a goal or issue. When a group of folks, even if they're spread wide apart by distance or identity, have a common goal with a clear vision, the work moves faster. A shared magic sigil helps to magnify and coordinate that effort more effectively than do singular or disorganized multiple workings.

My first shared magic sigil was the Power Sigil (page 162). I felt the need to aid and protect people in my immediate community and beyond, so I released the sigil into the world. I was blown away when so many people instantly connected with it. Basically, it went viral overnight and still keeps on trucking.

It has been an amazing experience to watch these sigils spread throughout the internet, especially to see who has shared them (and sometimes why) and to get a peek at how they are being used and how they are received. The majority of people seem to instantly embrace and use them. Then there are folks with differing political or magical views who get angry without really considering them. To which I say, the basic purpose for every one of these sigils is to support humanity, engage both emotions and logic, and encourage respectful understanding. I believe that's a baseline everyone should agree on.

In terms of making magic public and accessible, it's important to consider time and place. There are workings that by design and nature should be kept secret, allocated to the realm of silence and unspoken mystery. Their power vibrates within the folds of dark velvet, felt yet unseen. They shift and cause change like roots below the earth, moving a little at a time, slow and steady.

By that same measure, there are workings that are designed to be public, known, shown, and spoken. With every view or sharing, their power builds like a rising tide, making waves that cause change. They inspire, enthuse, and invigorate through their use and presence. They become an ocean that cannot be countered without great difficulty, because the waves can become endless, carving out a new landscape.

Both kinds of workings are necessary, and it's crucial to know the right time and place for each.

Shared magic sigils, by design, are meant to be public. They thrive in use and repetition; each use is a swelling wave of change. Others may seek to fight the wave, but the ocean cannot be stopped. The sigils work with the flow of humanity. The visual image, the method of physical application or metaphysical interaction, and most importantly the thoughts upon which the symbol was created all help unlock and empower the sigil. They continue to work subliminally, behind the scenes, much like the operating system of a computer or phone. They help each of us consider what we treasure and how we can manifest change in our personal world and in turn affect the macrocosm. Little shifts of position, new inspirations, cracks of light filtering through: nothing too dramatic on the personal level, but still change that you can stand back and see as the mosaic comes together. That's the power of shared magic, and it can make quite a difference.

Participating in Shared Magic

If you're looking to work with an established shared magic sigil or similar working to aid your community or create social change, there are a few things you should consider first.

Discern

If you've come across a sigil, spell, or proposed working online that's geared toward community change or magical resistance, do your research. Sit down with it for a little while, see who and where it came from, and consider if the components, ingredients, and actions make sense not only for you but for the cause you're working for. Does it feel right to you, or is something off? Is there something you could modify to make it more focused? If not, keep looking, or better yet, create your own.

Apply

Magic starts with thought, but many spells and sigils benefit from physical interaction. Drawing or tracing them in some way really has an impact, especially when using shared magic sigils. People say to me, "But I'm not an artist." You don't have to be an artist—there's not going to be a critique of your work. The act of drawing, carving, anointing, painting, etc., is what connects the sigil in your mind, body, and spirit. Folks talk about "charging" a sigil. Well, you do precisely that and more when you recreate the sigil by hand (or with your eyes if you're unable to use your hands). You are aligning your mind, your hand, and your heart in between. You are focusing your will.

Also consider what magical application works best for the particular spell or sigil. If you're looking to protect a body or place, then the best way to do that is to physically apply the sigil. If you're looking to send energy to a cause, then working with candles, dancing the sigil, etc., can help.

Action

Community aid and assistance is important work that can have quite an impact when done correctly. It can help bring awareness, direct energy, provoke thought, and manifest change. But make sure you follow up with physical action as well, in whatever form you are able to. Working for change comes in many forms: donating, supporting, sharing verified information, having tough conversations, protesting, getting folks registered to vote, cooking meals, providing childcare, providing emotional, mental, or legal counsel, etc. How can you have an effect locally?

Amplify

If a working doesn't resonate with you, then of course you can create your own. But keep in mind that shared magic workings benefit from many practitioners working collectively. So check to see if there's something already present that you can work with to help boost the signal.

Make sure you're not confusing the message, losing sight of the goal, or diminishing the agency of others. For example, folks have said to me, "You should create a sigil for Black Lives Matter." While their suggestion may seem well-intentioned, I myself am not Black. I believe that direction should come from someone who has that lived experience *and* is a recognized spokesperson for Black Lives Matter. Another thing to consider is that a sigil condenses multiple ideas into a singular focus and works in subtle ways. BLACK LIVES MATTER *is* the culmination of many important concepts into one simple, vital message that needs to be as visible as possible. Technically, #blacklivesmatter *is* a kind of sigil. So check to see if your idea actually amplifies and supports those who are marginalized. Otherwise, you could be overshadowing their voices and confusing the message.

Remember
Keep in mind your message and your focus—again, this is magic! Lastly, working for change is a marathon, not a sprint. Even when the news has subsided, consider how you can continue to amplify the message, bring awareness to the cause, and keep weaving the pattern strong.

Misinformed Ideas about Public Sigils
When it comes to the occult, it often feels like everyone has an opinion about what you should and shouldn't do. When I first started releasing the shared magic sigils to help with magical resistance and community issues, it was fascinating to see what opinions and concerns some people had about them. They fall into three basic categories:

1. Magic shouldn't be public/shared.
2. The sigils could have ulterior motives tied into them.
3. Magic shouldn't be political.

While I understand where some of these folks are coming from, these ideas are largely ill-informed or narrow-minded. Let's look at why that is, so you have a better understanding of what's possible.

Occult means hidden or secret. I feel studying the occult is about uncovering the mysteries within—that's the hidden part. While secrecy and witchcraft have gone hand in hand due to fear of persecution, I don't necessarily believe that what we do *has* to always be secret—unless you are in a situation where you need to be in the proverbial broom closet, meaning if someone catches wind that you're a witch or magical practitioner, it could be used to discriminate against you, causing you to lose your job, housing, children, or even your life. Then, yes, it's best to keep a lid on the cauldron and be discreet, unless you have an excellent lawyer on retainer.

Some folks feel bringing magic out into the open ruins it or strips away the mystery. But that feels more like a scarcity fear or a desire to keep some things exclusive. You can describe the mysteries to someone, but they still must be experienced to be fully revealed. That's the essence of it. A lot of folks make money and acquire power by making things exclusive and hierarchical: "There are secrets that only we know, and you have to go through us to get them." *Occult* does not mean inaccessible, nor exclusive, hierarchical, or unobtainable. No one group holds all the keys and secrets.

There are folks who shake their heads at the photos of altars and spells on Instagram. The altar is a place of action and connection. It's a place to channel power, but it is not power itself. Spell ingredients help coordinate and direct power, but they are not the spell itself. You are the source, the common factor.

Now, there is something to be said about choosing whether to reveal your game plan or secret strategy, especially in the midst of conflict. So I recommend being mindful about which workings you choose to make public and what level of access you give to it. For example, I created a shielding sigil for a specific group of people to use that only they had access to. By keeping it to only those concerned, I drew less attention to those needing the shielding and helped them in what they needed to do.

The second concern about public sigils, that they could have ulterior motives tied into them, is one that I think reveals more about the person saying it than anything else. Before you use any sigil that's been created by someone else, you should have a solid sense of what it's all about. That's why

I find that a lot of the statement sigils simply do not give enough information. Oh, that's a love sigil? What kind of love? What did the creator have in mind when they made it, and how do you know that aligns with the type of love you're looking for?

With my shared magic sigils, the majority of them are co-created, and every single one includes a breakdown of what went into it. Sure, there's room for interpretation, but I think the guidelines are clear enough for most people to understand effectively.

As for the last concern about public sigils, that magic shouldn't be political, living is political. Where and how we live, the food we eat, where we work, our access to resources and more—it's all subject to politics. Politics is about how decisions are made, the power and status dynamics among individuals and groups, as well as the distribution of resources. It's part of living in a society. When we reduce the idea of politics down to "these guys versus those guys" and think we're not a part of it, we miss out on participating in what's happening in our neighborhoods, cities, states, and countries. It's not magical to give up our personal power and influence, expecting someone else to do the job. We can't just sit there looking at our own navel and expect the world to change. We are all interconnected.

Choosing an Effective Focus for a Sigil

When working with social justice issues and community focuses, it helps to look at the bigger picture to make the most effective sigil. Let's look at a couple different situations and how they could be approached. How you view the world and have formulated your code of ethics will certainly be a factor in what you choose to do in any of these situations. What I find is most helpful is to ask, "How is my/our time and energy best used in this situation, and who will receive the greatest benefit from the work?" I feel more pulled to lend support to those who need it and are working for change than to directly battle the people causing the problems.

- *A hurricane is coming:* Every time a major storm or similar event is forecast to hit, I see folks saying, "I'm going to hex that storm." It's a natural event, so what does that even mean? How is that supposed to work? You could try to change the path of the storm, but are you just making it someone else's problem? Another option is to diminish its strength, slowing it down and having it wear itself out before it makes landfall. However, this won't work for folks who are against doing any kind of weather magic, even though it's likely the best option if you have the time and energy. You could focus your attention on protecting the land and communities that are likely to fall in the storm's path. Reducing wind and flood damage, making evacuation possible (and affordable) for those who will be most affected, and working for there to be enough resources for everyone are all excellent considerations.

- *A law has been passed that violates a group's bodily autonomy or right to exist:* Again, the first knee-jerk response to this situation is "hex the lawmakers." Which, to be honest, isn't a terrible idea, but will that alone accomplish what actually needs to be done? The people being affected need help and support. A new law needs to be introduced and the old one needs to be struck down, which involves organization and raising awareness. Voters need to be educated so they have a better understanding of what and whom they are voting for, as well as empathy for those affected. Justice needs to be called upon. Multiple sigils might be a better idea, or at least ones that address all these issues more effectively.

It's natural to want to immediately go on the offensive to protect others. Sometimes that *is* the right course of action. But more often than not, we're leaving the folks who need the most protection in the dust when they need help the most. Consider the long-term effects: Is the work we're doing not only helping right now but also directing energy to the best possible results down the line? We can choose to do magical triage to cure immediate problems, because sometimes it's necessary, but we should also be planning accordingly for the future.

Know Your Circle

What should you keep in mind when crafting a shared magic sigil? In truth, the process of creating a shared magic sigil is not much different in structure than for a personal sigil, but you need to be able to expand your scale and scope. Working with multiple people, especially those with knowledge of and experience with the issue or goal, helps a great deal. Multiple voices and backgrounds helps to craft a more universal symbolic language while ensuring the solution is being seen from several angles and possible outcomes. A key factor in a shared magic sigil is that it not only creates a cohesive visual element that can be used collectively but also helps everyone get a clearer picture of what's necessary to achieve that goal.

Once the sigil is complete, you need to think about how to distribute it. Consider what methods will make it accessible to others, including instructional references to help others understand and work with it. When I share sigils on my blog, I try to include the workboard if possible, so folks can see how the words match up with the marks, in addition to seeing the end result. I also emphasize what went into each sigil and provide suggestions on how to use it, as you'll see in the collection of sigils found in the next chapter.

I get a lot of messages and emails from folks who tell me I "should" create a sigil for this issue or that thing. I have two things to say about that. First, the reason I write books like this and teach classes is so you can learn to do the work you need to do. I'm saying, "Here are the tools for you to use. Please use them."

The second thing is that sometimes those issues or things are something completely outside of my experience or frame of reference. It makes no sense for me to create the sigil on my own, because I have only a rough idea (if any idea at all) of what's necessary to help solve or relieve that issue. There needs to be a connection and a foundation established. I can, however, effectively co-create sigils with folks who are informed and are part of that place or group. If they guide the reason for the working and do the brainstorming, then I can assist with the design. If you feel strongly about that specific thing, then you're likely a more qualified candidate for the job.

So if you feel moved to help others out, I recommend that you have a connection to the issue and a solid understanding of what is needed. Ideally, you want to include the input of others from that group or place if you are not a part of it or have never been. You can also consider creating a more general sigil that could be applied to multiple places or people, without tying it to a specific group or place. If you're part of a group that could be a better ally to another group you're not a part of, then a better option might be to create a sigil focused on education, empathy, and understanding on the part of your peers toward that group.

Creating Sigils for Individuals

The task of creating sigils or magical art for other people on a smaller scale is similar to crafting shared magic sigils in some ways. This type of work is usually for someone you know or perhaps someone who wants to commission you to create something for them. Instead of crafting for a whole community or larger society goal, the focus is on an individual's needs or goals.

Technically, making a sigil for someone is not any different from doing a spell for someone else. You should have a solid understanding of what that person needs or wants. This can be easy to grasp if you're working directly with them, especially when they have approached you to do the thing. The same can't quite be said when you're doing the work unsolicited, which also wanders into questionable ethical territory for a lot of folks. On one hand, you might make a healing sigil for someone who is unable to advocate or do the work for themselves in that moment. On the other hand, you might be creating something for someone where you *think* you know what they need but you really don't. But maybe you really know the person, so it depends on your relationship with them and the purpose of the sigil.

It's up to you to decide where to draw your moral and ethical lines. If you're likely to light a candle for someone to help them (without their knowledge), then creating a sigil with the same purpose in mind isn't much different. If you already provide spellcrafting services for others as part of your business (crafting oils and tinctures, carving candles, assembling spell kits, etc.), then crafting sigils already aligns with this same frame of mind. Similarly, if you create custom artwork for others by commission, then making sigils is likely also in your wheelhouse.

If you have no experience doing *any* kind of custom work or creating usable products for others, then sigil-crafting might not be an ideal place to start. It might seem like easy money to do some drawings for others, but it takes skill and effort to provide a quality product consistently and on time. If you think it's no big deal to charge nothing for your services, you're even more likely to burn out and disappoint others.[38] Evaluate your own schedule, ability, and most importantly reasons behind offering this service before hanging out your sigil shingle to the world.

As a professional artist and designer, I occasionally do design sigils and create magical artwork for other people. While I write books and teach workshops with the goal that readers and students alike will be inspired to create on their own, I recognize that some people prefer to collaborate to get their desired result. So when my schedule allows and if their idea resonates with me, I may take on their project. Technically I also do the same kind of outsourcing for tasks and goals that I don't have the time, skill, or resources for. For example, I have worked with Lyra of Spiral Moon Herbcraft to create custom oils because I trust her sense of scent, feel, and high-quality approach to create potent anointing oils.[39] I collect art and decks from other artists because I appreciate their style. While I have made my own incense, I love supporting my friends who do it professionally. I believe that most of my art and design clients are taking the same mental approach, more or less.

So how do you go about crafting a sigil or piece of magical art for someone else? I already talked about my artmaking process in the section "Imbuing Art with Intent" back in chapter 4, but there are some specific things I need to sort out before creating art for someone else:

---

38. If you offer services to the general public, even if you compartmentalize it as "practice," you should be charging for your time. If you just want to practice learning a new skill, then craft for yourself or form a group of friends to work with to build your familiarity with the task *and* working with others.
39. View Lyra's work at https://spiralmoonherbcraft.com.

1. First I find out what they are looking for in a sigil or piece of artwork. Aside from the business aspects of size, budget, timing, and media necessities (miniature spell painting, sigil, altar piece, pen and ink, etc.), I ask if they have a goal or purpose for the art.

2. If it's a sigil, I request that they write a short paragraph or make a list of what they wish to accomplish with the sigil and what success looks like for them. If the sigil is for a deity or spirit, I inquire about what myths they are drawn to, what their relationship with the deity or spirit is like, and if there is any existing art that captures how they see that deity.

3. Once I have a good idea of what they're looking for, I prepare my materials, do any necessary sketches, set up any visual guides I may need, and focus on the person as I work. The feeling of focus is very similar to how I "tap into" folks I do tarot readings for. I take myself out of the equation (except as a medium) and turn my attention to their rhythms and patterns. For sigils, I don't show them the work until it's done. For paintings and drawings, I tend to send in-progress shots, mainly because I'm excited and like to share the process with them.

Once the work is done, it's delivered on the terms agreed upon. As a business note, small projects like digitally delivered sigils are paid for in advance. Bigger projects like paintings usually require a 50 percent deposit and don't ship until the balance is paid. It may seem uncouth to talk about the financial bits, but money represents the energy exchange happening here. My time is valuable and art materials are expensive. Not only do *you* need to value yourself, but numerous studies have shown that most people apply greater worth to things they pay for versus freebies.

The Business of Branding

When you start a new business or decide to take your existing business in a new direction, it's a smart idea to have a business plan. A business plan is a document that outlines your business's future objectives, as well as strategies for achieving those goals. You can review and update your business plan periodically to see how well your goals have been met or if they have changed or shifted. Right there you already have steps 1 and 2 of the Sigil Witchery method established, so why not take it to the next step and use your business plan to create a sigil logo?

The benefit of using a sigil for creating your logo/brand design is that it amplifies your vision. You can use the resulting sigil on signs, business cards, product packaging, etc. Every time it's seen or used, it's emphasizing the pattern of success and prosperity you envision for your business.

You don't have to make the sigil your primary logo, but could instead subtly incorporate it into your materials, or use elements of it in your logo/marketing design, or simply keep it to yourself to do other kind of magical work with it.

TECH TIP: THE *LOGOS* OF LOGOS

Creating a successful logo isn't easy. There's a reason why some graphic designers make excellent money crafting just logos for others. The brainstorming and basic design part of the sigil process can help you explain to a designer what it is you're looking for in a logo, what elements are important to you, and what your overall vision is for your business. If you do want to create a logo from your sigil, here are some good guidelines to keep in mind:

- Keep it simple. You want an image that stands out, isn't too complicated, and "reads" easily to most people.

- Stand back and look at it. Flip it upside down and backward. Does it unintentionally look like something else? Other people are very helpful in determining if your beautiful sigil accidentally looks like a Sheela-na-gig or a sad boot.

- Play with size. Can you still tell what it is on a small business card, as well how it might look on a six-foot banner?

- Check the message. Does it feel like the image gets your message across? Is it your business embodied in a few marks?

- Try different color options on light and dark backgrounds.

- Always scan in or create your work at a high resolution—a minimum of 300 dpi. When you go to make that six-foot banner, you'll thank me.

- Allow for flexibility. Logos can grow and change over time. Just do a quick search on the logo history of Pepsi or Starbucks to see what I mean.

Magic on the Go

Murals, sculptures, and big art installations are fantastic in how they transform spaces. They can certainly possess several layers of powerful magic. But they're place-specific and often time-consuming to create. They're also not typically mobile or easily transported.

On the other hand, a well-designed sigil is exceptionally mobile and can be created in a matter of moments or minutes. Sigils can be quickly drawn with chalk, pen, or marker, then easily stenciled or printed onto a sticker and affixed somewhere.

In chapter 1 of *Sigil Witchery*, "A History of Mark Making," I spend some time discussing graffiti and tagging. Humans have been making unsanctioned marks for thousands of years—you'll find evidence of graffiti all over the world. Whether these marks are considered vandalism, street art, or a means of coded communication, there's something magical about marks made in liminal spaces with occult intent. Whether they are carved or painted to last or will be gone with the next rainstorm, they draw our eyes and fascinate our minds. We ponder our relationship to the creator, and at the same time we join an audience of many, absorbing or trying to uncover the meaning behind the mark.

Although Shepard Fairey graduated eight years before I did from Rhode Island School of Design, while I was a student there you could still find his iconic "André the Giant Has a Posse" stickers posted all over campus. According to the Obey Giant website:

> The OBEY sticker campaign can be explained as an experiment in Phenomenology. Heidegger describes Phenomenology as "the process of letting things manifest themselves." Phenomenology attempts to enable people to see clearly something that is right before their eyes but obscured; things that are so taken for granted that they are muted by abstract observation.
>
> The first aim of phenomenology is to reawaken a sense of wonder about one's environment. The OBEY sticker attempts to stimulate curiosity and bring people to question both the sticker and their relationship with their surroundings.[40]

Sigils and symbols in strange places definitely tap into that sense of wonder and curiosity. But while Fairey's sticker is designed to have no meaning, sigils obviously are. Where and how we place them can add to the meaning, as well as affect how others may receive them. Sometimes our goal is to place the sigils not in plain sight, but to camouflage them to be part of their surroundings. So one thing to consider is if the sigil is meant to be seen for a long time, only present for a few moments or days, or essentially present but invisible for as long as possible. Which option is right for the sigil depends on the purpose of the sigil and why you're placing it there.

---

40. "Manifesto," Obey Giant, https://obeygiant.com/articles/manifesto.

TECH TIP: APPLYING SIGILS TO ENVIRONMENTS

The way I look at it, magic on the go can be designed to be semipermanent or ephemeral. I can't advocate damaging public or personal property for obvious legal reasons, so it's up to you to decide what's appropriate. I do ask that you respect the environment and don't damage natural habitats or historical sites. Here are a few suggestions for each method.

Semipermanent methods:

- Waterproof/vinyl stickers
- Carved into stone or wood
- Drawn in wet plaster, clay, or concrete
- Permanent alcohol or oil-based markers

Ephemeral methods:

- Drawn in dirt, sand, or gravel
- Dry-erase markers
- Charcoal
- Chalk
- Paper stickers

Whether you choose to keep your work personal and private or public and open to be shared depends on you and the purpose of your work. I hope that as we wrap things up here, you have a better understanding of what the differences can mean for your art and your practice.

Chapter 6
Sharing Sigils

Artists are the shamans, the priests and priestesses, the magicians of society.
—Audrey Flack, *Art & Soul*

This chapter contains a reference gallery of the fifty most popular shared magic sigils I have created myself or helped to create, including the history and breakdown of each sigil and suggested uses. Why have I included all these sigils when I have also said that making your own sigils is often the best course of action? I'm glad you asked, as there are several important reasons. First, these sigils help you see how and why they were constructed, which in turn can inspire your own practice. Second, they set a model for creating and distributing your own shared magic sigils through the explanation of what went into them and how to use them effectively. Third, it's always handy to have a resource of ready-made sigils that you can easily understand and work with—whether for yourself or with a group. Definitely *do* make your own sigils, but also feel free to use these as a guide and work with the ones that call to you.

I have separated the sigils into categories for easy reference, though several of them could easily work in more than one category. I have not included sigils that are highly specific to certain events (such as a festival sigil) or locations (created to help that specific town/city). While some of the sigils included here may contain elements of inspiration from the place where they were curated, they all have a certain universality to them—that is, they can be used beyond a certain situation or place. Also, the suggestions for use are exactly that: suggestions. If you are inspired to work with any of these sigils in some other way that makes sense to you, then by all means pursue that inspiration.[41] Keep in mind that these sigils aren't meant to replace mundane action, but are meant to lend or add support to their intended goal. That means combining both magical and mundane efforts when necessary—as is true with any form of spellcraft.

My thanks to all the students across the world who have co-created sigils with me in workshops. One of my favorite parts of these workshops is to be able to bring the process to life and provide the opportunity for everyone to participate in their own way.

Some Notes about Design

The majority of the sigils presented here have workboard images you can study online. If you search my Patheos blog for the sigil name or use the #sigil tag in the archive search, you should be able to easily locate the sigil's post, which may include a shot of the workshop whiteboard or sketch pad.[42]

You may also notice some similarity between some designs. Often it's because the sigils are related in their goal and/or share base elements. Also, when sigils are co-crafted in a workshop, they are not being compared to previous examples but are made in the moment.

A Note about Legal Usage

The majority of these sigils were released on my blog with a Creative Commons Attribution-NonCommercial-ShareAlike 4.0 International license.[43] This means you are free to use and share a sigil with proper attribution and only for noncommercial means. You can also adapt the image as long as you make it available under the same terms (attributed, noncommercial use, share-alike).

---

41. Use these shared sigils as long as it doesn't violate the legal usage bits—see the next section!
42. Laura Tempest Zakroff, *A Modern Traditional Witch* (blog), https://www.patheos.com/blogs/tempest/.
43. For a full breakdown of what a CC4 license covers, see the description at the very end of the book.

Health and Healing Sigils

These sigils are designed to aid in health and healing—not just physically, but emotionally and mentally as well.

Anti-Burnout Sigil

Summary

This sigil helps to bring a sense of renewal when facing difficult times and situations.

Location and Date of Creation

The Raven's Wing Magical Co., Oakland, CA, June 28, 2018

What Elements Went into the Sigil

- Abundance (in terms of what energy and resources are needed to combat burnout)
- Maintain a sense of balance as needed
- Amplify good health
- A pilot light that inspires, cleanses, and invigorates
- Protection
- Allow for rooting, grounding (of ideas, of mind and body)
- A focus on other, the umbrella, community

Anti-Burnout Sigil

Suggestions for Use

You can wear this sigil, share it, draw it in healing colors, place it on your altar, or put it where folks need to be renewed and refreshed. This would be a good sigil to "consume" via food or beverage.

Balanced Health Sigil

Summary

This sigil is designed to help us get through the dark part of the year in good physical, emotional, mental, and environmental health.

Location and Date of Creation

Arts & Crafts: Botanica & Occult Shop, Pittsburgh, PA, September 30, 2019

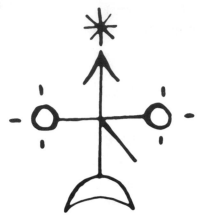

Balanced Health Sigil

What Elements Went into the Sigil

- Good mental/emotional state of being
- Promote physical wellness/anti-sickness
- Resilience
- Provide a supportive environment
- Build relationships
- Release of unnecessary emotional/mental weight

Suggestions for Use

This sigil is ideal for use from the fall equinox to the spring equinox. It can be anointed on the body, marked in the home, or placed on a candle (white, pink, or yellow is suggested).

Encompassing Heart Sigil

Summary

This is a sigil of transition to bring a sense of healing, comfort, and vision as we move through the end of the year into the next. It helps close the distance between hearts and spirits alike.

Location and Date of Creation

Virtual workshop, December 12, 2020

What Elements Went into the Sigil

- Comfort, peace, and to be able to be lighthearted
- Closing the distance between friends/family/loved ones, enhancing connection
- Healing (inside and out)
- Focus on health, being community-minded, clarity in embracing that mindfulness, caring for one another
- Replenishing energy, creating a positive cycle, transformation, love moving in and out
- Protection and security to provide a foundation
- Leaving the past year's energy behind (the negative aspects) while taking wisdom with us to guide

Encompassing Heart Sigil

Suggestions for Use

Place this sigil on a candle (white, gold, or warm color tones), apply to the body with anointing oil that stimulates a heart focus, set on your altar or hearth, use as a focus/inspiration for movement, or set with photos of those you miss.

Healing of Wounds Sigil

Summary

This sigil can be used for many kinds of wounds: spiritual, emotional, mental, and / or physical.

Healing of Wounds Sigil

Location and Date of Creation

Sacred Hearth Sanctuary, Reno, NV, September 21, 2019

What Elements Went into the Sigil

- Foster patience
- Aid in recovery
- Draw prosperity
- Focus on healthy growth
- Release of pain
- Receptive to helpful change
- Encourage stability
- Help to process grief
- Bring peace

Suggestions for Use

The type of working that is appropriate for this sigil depends on the kind of healing required. You could center this sigil on a part of the body in need of healing, administered via poppet, candle, or another form of sympathetic magic. It could also be carved into candles, applied with oils, tattooed, hennaed, placed on your altar, etc. While the first instinct might be to apply it to bodies, this sigil can also be used to heal places and sites.

Good Health Sigil (Immunity Booster Sigil)

Summary

This sigil is designed to help aid in the processes that contribute to sustainable good health.

Location and Date of Creation

Created by the author, March 8, 2020

What Elements Went into the Sigil

- Protection
- Responsible mindfulness
- Community-conscious
- Promote cleanliness and good hygiene
- Minimize transmission
- Sustained good health
- Enough resources for all (prevention and treatment)
- Affordable access to those resources for everyone
- Focus on lungs
- Calm, let wisdom and common sense guide

Good Health Sigil

Suggestions for Use

Post this sigil in public places where transmission of contagious diseases can increase (meeting rooms, bathrooms, kitchens), as well as places where promoting excellent sanitary habits benefits everyone. Carve into soap for washing the body or apply to health-boosting tincture containers, water bottles, and other personal cups. Anoint the body with it using oils. Place on candles to help focus energy on those who especially need additional protection.

A Sigil for Managing Panic

Summary

This sigil is designed to help bring calm and clarity to our minds, bodies, and spirits, as well as bring calm to the larger community.

Location and Date of Creation

Virtual workshop, April 22, 2020

What Elements Went into the Sigil

A Sigil for Managing Panic

- Revelation of truth
- Clarity/clear signal
- Movement of information in the correct direction
- Healing/health-focused
- Foster critical thinking/discernment
- Encourage positive action (things that help, not hurt)
- Community-mindful—being more conscious that we're all interconnected; looking out for everyone, not just the self
- Increase compassion and empathy

Suggestions for Use

Use this sigil for meditation and as a focus for breath exercises. Draw it in the earth around your home, imbue it into a calming beverage, carve it into soap, anoint your body with it using a calming oil (lavender or a similar oil), or place it on candles (whatever color is calming for you).

Survivor Support Sigil

Summary

The purpose of this sigil is to give multiple levels of support to survivors—amplifying the power within while also creating a more supportive community in the process.

Location and Date of Creation

The Curious Cauldron, Fort Myers, FL, October 25, 2018

What Elements Went into the Sigil

To ensure that survivors…

- are listened to/heard
- are believed/seen
- are surrounded by safety
- are met with empathy
- can facilitate self-healing
- gain strength
- are given justice

Survivor Support Sigil

Suggestions for Use

This sigil can be used in personal healing rituals and self-care workings (anointing the body, meditation, tattoo work, etc.), but it can also be used by the larger community to help generate healing for survivors. Use it in protests and put it in correspondence regarding rights, legislation, and funding to aid survivors and to promote education.

A Sigil to Defeat Breast Cancer

Summary

This sigil is designed to aid in the battle against breast cancer, especially for the individual going through the ordeal themselves. I created this sigil for a friend in 2020 and then shared it with several more friends who were diagnosed with breast cancer in late 2021 to early 2022.

I never knew my paternal grandmother, as she died from breast cancer in her late thirties, and it's also been present in my maternal line—so breast cancer is a very personal issue for me. If you're dealing with another form of cancer, consider the list below and what areas the cancer affects. From there you have a guide for creating your own specific sigil.

Location and Date of Creation

Created by the author, New England, summer of 2020

What Elements Went into the Sigil

- Focus of energy on breasts and affected tissues/organs
- Strength and endurance
- Emotional and mental support
- Healing and steadfast recovery
- Reclamation of body
- Balance and rejuvenation
- Positive outcome

A Sigil to Defeat
Breast Cancer

Suggestions for Use

This sigil can be applied directly to the body (with blessed water, anointing oil, temporary markers for the skin, etc.) or worn on the body in other ways (clothing, jewelry, etc.). It can be carved into a candle (white, pink, or light blue is suggested) or placed on an altar or mobile device for meditation.

Creativity and Movement Sigils

These sigils promote creativity and positive motion, bringing inspiration and change.

Emergence Sigil

Emergence Sigil

Summary

This sigil aids the human psyche as we work to get past difficult times, emerging beyond them more empowered, hopeful, and inspired.

Location and Date of Creation

Virtual workshop, April 27, 2021

What Elements Went into the Sigil

- Stability and security
- Mental peace/peace of mind
- Blossoming or unfurling
- Foster equity and social justice in our communities
- Strength as we move forward
- Able to move past fears and obstacles to truth
- Bringing the wisdom of what we've learned with us/carrying lessons forward
- Health
- Embodying truth while being future-minded, maintain/build hope
- Building community together

Suggestions for Use

Use this sigil as a community focus in virtual or health-minded physical rituals, carve it into a candle (white or blue is suggested) and place on your altar (especially on your hearth altar if you have one), or bless your home with it, drawing it with consecrated water and earth.

A Sigil to Feed the Body and Soul

Summary
This sigil not only addresses the body and soul of human beings but also recognizes the larger body and spirit of the earth and nature that we are also a part of. We wanted to create something that also addresses agricultural and farming needs (to literally feed and sustain folks), works with the environment itself, and taps into mental, emotional, and spiritual needs.

A Sigil to Feed the Body and Soul

Location and Date of Creation
Virtual workshop, March 28, 2020

What Elements Went into the Sigil
- Beneficial abundance (in attune with nature and needs)
- Rebirth and transformation
- Growth (crops, people, etc.)
- Awareness of what is needed (to aid in creating change)
- Personal agency and accountability
- Generosity (to give and receive freely to aid each other)
- Recognition of our connection with nature
- Endurance and resilience
- Stimulating support for necessary changes
- Embracing simplicity and releasing what is unneeded, unnecessary, or harmful

Suggestions for Use
This sigil works well when applied directly to a place, so you can draw it on the ground, paint or draw it on a rock and expose it to the elements, use it to guide a garden, water the earth with it, etc. You can also adorn or anoint the body with it or place it on a green, yellow, or gold candle.

Unstuck Sigil

Summary

This sigil is ideal for those times when you feel that things just aren't moving or flowing like they normally do. Use it to stimulate inspiration or move along matters that seem to be dragging.

Unstuck Sigil

Location and Date of Creation

Radiance Herbs & Massage, Olympia, WA, September 18, 2018

What Elements Went into the Sigil

- Stimulate movement
- Promote creativity
- Draw inspiration
- Empowerment
- Instill a sense of freedom
- Joy/happiness
- Foster connection

Suggestions for Use

Consider using this sigil in conjunction with the lunar calendar, working with the waning moon to remove blockages or using the waxing moon to push things along. Take this sigil to the water and draw it where the waves can wash it away, or draw it on a leaf and release it into running water.

Uplifting Sigil

Summary

This sigil is designed to uplift your spirit when you're feeling down and help you remember the beautiful aspects of living.

Location and Date of Creation

The Veiled Crow, Cranston, RI, February 5, 2020

What Elements Went into the Sigil

- Increase stamina
- Energy to move forward toward what is worthwhile
- Stimulate happiness
- Amplify hope
- Clear vision (to see the path ahead)
- Share the wealth (helping to uplift and support others)
- Faith/trust in the universe

Uplifting Sigil

Suggestions for Use

You can wear this sigil, draw it in appropriate places to lift your spirits, use it for blessings, or tattoo it. You could carve it into a candle (white, yellow, or light blue is suggested), anoint your body with it using an invigorating oil, or add it to an altar or vision board for help in focusing on positive things.

Luck and Prosperity Sigils

These sigils are designed to attract good fortune and prosperity.

Business Success Sigil

Summary

This sigil was crafted in a workshop that was largely made up of independent business folks, so business success was an obvious focus. It is ideal for small/indie/community businesses.

Business Success Sigil

Location and Date of Creation

The Cauldron Black, Salem, MA, August 5, 2019

What Elements Went into the Sigil

- Self-sufficient
- Sustainable/steady growth
- Fashionable/attractive/relevant = recognizable/memorable to others
- Clear reception of concept, signal being heard by target market
- Ethical, responsible, accountable
- Collaboration/community/networking
- Prosperity

Suggestions for Use

This sigil can be situated in your place of business or workspace, used in conjunction with offerings to related deities and spirits (such as Fortuna), used to anoint points of entry, or inserted digitally in websites and other marketing materials.

Good Luck Sigil

Summary

This sigil is designed to help bring good luck your way (or to someone or someplace else).

Location and Date of Creation

Finding Avalon, Camden, DE, October 9, 2018

What Elements Went into the Sigil

- Good health
- Sustainable wealth
- Open to opportunity
- Focus/sight/clarity
- Protection (to maintain luck)
- Initiative (to follow through on opportunities)

Good Luck Sigil

Suggestions for Use

Anoint or draw this sigil on the body, make it into something wearable (like jewelry or a patch, or painted on a coat, purse, or book bag), draw it on homes and vehicles, carve it into a candle (green, rainbow, or white is suggested), place it on a reusable water bottle, or infuse it into your coffee/tea.

Time and Place Sigils

These sigils are designed to aid in issues of place as well as time—sometimes both at once. *Place* can be as literal as where we are living physically or it can be more abstract, like where we are mentally, emotionally, or spiritually.

A Sigil to Foster Stability

Summary

Within the word *stability* we find *ability*—the power to be able to make the next move, to plan for the future or at least hold your ground in the present. Stability helps provide a foundation for us to build upon, to discover solace, to be able to heal or find respite.

Location and Date of Creation

Virtual workshop, July 25, 2020

What Elements Went into the Sigil

- Promote good health
- Provide for steady/stable prosperity and resources
- Peace (found through justice/root growth)
- Supporting upcoming generations/building a worthy legacy
- Balance
- Thriving growth
- Ease of transition/adaptability
- Resilience and strength

A Sigil to Foster Stability

Suggestions for Use

Draw or carve this sigil on a candle (green, blue, brown, or white is suggested), use it as a meditation focus, or draw it outside or even within your place of residence (can be done visibly with chalk or invisibly with blessed water, incense, etc.).

Housing Crisis Sigil

Summary
This sigil is designed to aid in providing safe, affordable, and desirable housing.

Location and Date of Creation
The Green Man, Los Angeles, CA, June 24, 2018

What Elements Went into the Sigil
- Provide home spaces for people
- Increase affordable housing for all
- Ensure the spaces are safe and welcoming
- Humane treatment, recognition of humanity, reducing the problems that can lead to homelessness/being unhoused
- Building a better community that supports all of its members
- Create/promote housing that helps with the flow of traffic, accessible to transit/public transportation
- Make resources available (physical, emotional, and mental needs)
- Focus on building stability/structure

Housing Crisis Sigil

Suggestions for Use
This is an ideal location-placed sigil. You can carve it into a candle to help focus energy on the cause, chalk it onto walls and spaces of affected places, use it to aid legislation, use it to attract development that is beneficial for the people of a place, or put it on protest signs.

Needs Met Sigil

Summary

Sometimes there are many facets of an issue that need to be addressed ASAP. This sigil lends focus and energy to help those needs get met quickly and effectively.

Location and Date of Creation

Virtual workshop, March 20, 2020

Needs Met Sigil

What Elements Went into the Sigil

- Minimize threats, reduce harm
- Utilize equinox energy to tap into a sense of balance, of moving from dark into light
- Protection for the protectors—those folks on the front lines helping people
- Aid with mental health, anti-anxiety
- Foster compassion and love
- Recognition of connection
- Needs being met
- Reminder to practice self-care/care for others
- Increase ingenuity/resourcefulness
- Effective quickly/as fast as possible

Suggestions for Use

This sigil is ideal as a focus for both personal and community ritual work. For candle work, a basic white candle is fine, but use whatever color you feel drawn to or have available.

A Sigil for Time Management

Summary

This sigil is ideal if you're looking to stay on task with projects, find a healthy balance between work, play, and rest, craft a functional schedule, or stick to a deadline. It's also helpful if you need some assistance with directing your focus and attention.

Location and Date of Creation

Soul Journey, Butler, NJ, October 16, 2018

What Elements Went into the Sigil

- Having motivation
- Maintaining focus
- Being goal-oriented
- Realistic expectations/mindset
- Healthy approach/habits for managing time
- Sense of balance

A Sigil for Time Management

Suggestions for Use

This is a great sigil to use to watch over your workspace, be it your office, the kitchen, a desk area, a studio, the garden—basically wherever you need to get work done or better manage your time to address things you need to do. You can also apply it to a candle to light while you work on a project. Consider drawing or tracing it as part of a morning meditation before officially starting your day.

Death and Transition Sigils

These sigils deal with death, crossing over, and working with the deceased.

Ancestral Connection Sigil

Summary

This sigil is designed to aid you in making contact and communing with the deceased. It was especially crafted with the goal of bringing wisdom from our ancestors into the future.

Location and Date of Creation

Virtual workshop, October 19, 2021

What Elements Went into the Sigil

- Connection, reading through the veil safely (per the user's perception and understanding of the veil)
- Drawing wisdom and strength from the ancestors to bring forward into the future
- Aid in personal growth
- Building community growth
- Providing vision and clarity
- Healing and understanding
- Release from perpetuating harmful cycles

Ancestral Connection Sigil

Suggestions for Use

Use this sigil in meditation and ritual when honoring the deceased, the beloved and Mighty Dead, etc. Add the sigil to your ancestral / Hallows / Samhain altar, apply it to a candle (white, black, red, or silver is recommended—follow your intuition), or place it near or on a container of incense that has been blended to honor the dead.

Psychopomp Sigil

Summary

Psychopomps are beings who are responsible for escorting newly deceased souls from Earth to the afterlife. This sigil is designed to ease the passing of those who are dying or deceased, as well as comfort those left behind.

Psychopomp Sigil

Location and Date of Creation

Virtual workshop, April 23, 2020

What Elements Went into the Sigil

- Peace
- Lessening of fear (of death/transition)
- Aid in crossing the threshold/passing the barrier between life and death
- Love
- Release of spirit
- Forgiveness, letting go
- Comfort, easing of pain
- Emphasize connection
- For the dying to know they are not alone
- Guidance and direction

Suggestions for Use

Combine this sigil with mugwort workings (tinctures, infusions, oils, etc.), place it on a candle (light or dark blue, white, silver, or gold are all good options), add it to a memorial altar or an altar for the dying, or incorporate it into a poppet or similar working to aid in a peaceful transition or perform memorial or funerary rites by proxy.

Samhain Sigil

Summary

This sigil incorporates many elements that are accessible and useful for doing ancestor rituals as well as mediumship work at this time of year. Used with focus and intention, it can act as a responsible and conscious doorway that enables communication and connection during the dark half of the year.

Samhain Sigil

Location and Date of Creation

Enchanted Earth, Dunedin, FL, October 26, 2018

What Elements Went into the Sigil

- Protection from unwanted/undesirable spirits and entities
- Aid in communication with the other side
- Enhance second sight/psychic abilities
- Allow for compassion and forgiveness for those who have passed on
- Blessing energy
- Increase connection
- Support a door/gateway between worlds/minds during ritual work
- Based in love
- Build/allow for comprehension and understanding messages that are given

Suggestions for Use

You can use this sigil for your own rituals, draw it on a candle, place it on an altar, use it for protection while working with ancestors and other spirits, etc. As you can see, it does have characteristics of a literal door or gateway, so this is likely not a sigil that you want to leave around all year round.

Sigils to Protect People

These sigils focus on aiding or assisting specific groups of people.

Border Sigil (A Sigil to Resolve Border Issues and Facilitate Healing)

Border Sigil

Summary

This sigil is designed to help improve the humanitarian situations that happen at the borders between countries and foster more understanding and connection.

Location and Date of Creation

Tree of Life Metaphysical Books and Gifts, San Diego, CA, June 23, 2018

What Elements Went into the Sigil

- Lend strength to those who need it
- Promote peace
- Open (applies to hearts, minds, legal / safe crossing, asylum)
- Recognition of humanity
- Aid in healing
- Reunite families
- Foster community and connection
- Love
- Awakening to the issues for informed progress

Suggestions for Use

Draw this sigil in appropriate places or carve it into a candle to help focus energy on the cause. Share it with folks who live or work near a border, are seeking safe passage across country lines, or are in danger of being unfairly or illegally retained.

A Sigil to Protect Protesters (ICE Sigil)

Summary

This sigil is also referred to as the ICE Sigil, as it was first created to aid in the protection of those protesting ICE as well as detainees, but it applies to all protesters demonstrating for causes involving human rights as well as environmental protection.

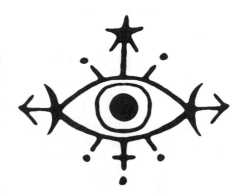

A Sigil to Protect Protesters

Location and Date of Creation

The Raven's Wing Magical Co., Portland, OR, June 30, 2018

What Elements Went into the Sigil

- Prevent the arrest of protesters and those who would be detained
- Provide stamina for protesters
- Good weather for protesters
- Ensure that their message is seen/visible/heard and has an impact
- Resilience
- Fuel hope

Suggestions for Use

You can wear this sigil, share it, draw it in appropriate places, make signs of it, or use it for blessings and other forms of protection. You don't have to be physically out there protesting to use this sigil—you can use it to lend support to others and bring more focused energy to the situation, guided toward a positive and powerful solution.

A Sigil to Defend Transfolx

Summary

This sigil is designed to protect and defend the bodies and rights of transfolx.

Location and Date of Creation

Atlanta workshop, October 27, 2018

What Elements Went into the Sigil

- Protect transfolx
- Stand up for them
- Speak up to defend them
- Help educate the world
- Bring greater comprehension, understanding, and empathy
- Foster inclusion
- Aid in healing

Suggestions for Use

A Sigil to Defend Transfolx

You can wear this sigil, share it, draw it in appropriate places, use it for blessings, tattoo it, etc. It can be used to defend one's home, body, or community place.

A Sigil for the Protection of Transgender Rights

Summary

Similar to the Transfolx Sigil, this sigil is focused on rights and legislation. These two sigils can be used together or separately.

Location and Date of Creation

Scarlet Woman Lodge, Austin, TX, November 3, 2018

What Elements Went into the Sigil

- Promote understanding
- Command respect, positive attention
- Increase compassion
- Opportunity for education
- Strength
- Foster equality
- Build acceptance
- Lend protection

A Sigil for the Protection of Transgender Rights

Suggestions for Use

You can wear this sigil, share it, draw it in appropriate places, use it in places where rights are being violated or in danger, or use it in postcards, legislation, and other materials to educate folks. It's a front-line sigil for helping to defend trans rights, which are human rights.

Power Sigil

Summary

This sigil is for all those who need protection and guidance. We can summon its power to help us navigate our way safely to our destination.

Power Sigil

Location and Date of Creation

Created by the author, November 9, 2016, Seattle, WA

What Elements Went into the Sigil

- Protection for those in crisis or need
- Combination of the elements that make us all up: earth, air, fire, water, and spirit
- Recognition of the other
- Balance and equality
- Revelation of the seed of truth, directing it outward to find purchase
- Calm within the storm
- Recognize personal power
- Honoring the body
- Foster hope
- Facing and banishing fears
- Stimulate action that creates and supports change

Suggestions for Use

You can make this sigil into a talisman, tattoo it on your body, trace it during meditation, place it on a candle, wear it on clothing—whatever helps you activate it.

Refugee Safeguard Sigil

Summary

This sigil is designed to help direct aid, resources, and positive attention to those in need of immediate assistance as well as healing and resolution.

Location and Date of Creation

Virtual workshop, August 17, 2021

What Elements Went into the Sigil

- Escape to safety (if escape is necessary), give direction
- Nest/safe spaces/nourishing safe places and resources
- Establish security and foster strength
- Compassion and love
- Foster connections (family + world)
- Protection—of the body, but also of traditions and memories
- Respect and understanding
- Courage
- Health
- Education (access and expansion)
- Freedom

Refugee Safeguard Sigil

Suggestions for Use

Use this sigil as a community/group focus in ritual to help bring attention to the plight of refugees and clear the path for the resources they need. Use it to bless places that are aiding refugees.

Reproductive Rights Sigil

Summary

This sigil is designed to aid in the protection of reproductive rights wherever they are under threat.

Location and Date of Creation

Virtual workshop, October 25, 2021

Reproductive Rights Sigil

What Elements Went into the Sigil

- Protection of rights, services, people
- Increased access to safe and legal procedures
- Health-minded focus
- Fact-based education about bodies, sex, pregnancy
- Body autonomy / respecting the sovereign self
- Removal of obstacles to safe / legal treatment for all
- Legalization secured permanently, not to be threatened or overturned

Suggestions for Use

Use this sigil in protests (on signs and bodies), draw it in appropriate places (health services, education centers), put it on candles, or use it in correspondence to health and legal institutions.

Resilient Sigil for Women

Summary

This is a sigil to protect, heal, and acknowledge all women.

Location and Date of Creation

MagikCraft, Durham, NC, October 18, 2018

What Elements Went into the Sigil

- Healing trauma
- Protection for women
- Strength to be resilient
- Wisdom (of self and community)
- Hope for change
- Community support
- Love (of self, of women)
- Believe/belief (to believe women, to hold the belief of women's power in all of us)

Resilient Sigil for Women

Suggestions for Use

You can use this sigil to lend support to all women and bring more understanding to women's issues and needs, as well as focus power and strength to protecting women's rights everywhere. It can be worn, drawn in appropriate places, placed on protest signs, put on candles, used for blessings and other forms of protection, or drawn on the body using essential oils.

A Sigil for the Protection of the Vulnerable

A Sigil for the Protection
of the Vulnerable

Summary

This sigil was created to help those dealing with abuse and to guide them to resources and possibilities that will enable a safe and healthy path. It acts not only as a shield but also as a beacon of hope for the future.

Location and Date of Creation

Virtual workshop, April 11, 2020

What Elements Went into the Sigil

- Being safe at home—physical safety
- Peace of mind—emotional and mental safety
- Able to have good boundaries
- Strength
- Aid to help plan for the future
- Access to resources to bring about change/gather support
- Maintaining safe connections/know that you are not alone
- Healthy outlets
- Mental clarity/discernment (to see the situation for what it is and devise a successful and safe exit strategy)

Suggestions for Use

Anoint the body daily with this sigil using an oil that also aids in protection, carve it into soap to wash the body, place it on a candle (light blue, white, purple, silver, or gold are all good options), draw it with smoke or blessed water around the focused living area (wherever the vulnerable person is living or being affected or is being kept safe), or use it in a binding spell.

Shekhinah Sigil

Summary

This sigil was created to protect Jewish folks and spaces that are sacred to them. Shekhinah is an English transliteration of a Hebrew word meaning "dwelling" or "settling," and denotes the dwelling or settling of the divine presence of God.

Location and Date of Creation

Created by the author, November 1, 2018, New Orleans, LA

What Elements Went into the Sigil

- Star of David, representing Jewishness plus "as above, so below"
- Sending out protection
- Amplify truth and wisdom
- Illumination
- Preservation of traditions and rising generations
- Community-centered
- Focus and guidance

Shekhinah Sigil

Suggestions for Use

This sigil can be drawn on bodies and places to protect them or carved into candles for focusing and blessing work. It can be stitched, painted, anointed—whatever you feel the need to do.

Communication Sigils

These sigils help improve communication as well as clarity of vision.

Clarity for the Next Step Sigil

Summary

This sigil helps to deal with uncertainty, especially if you're in a position to be wondering, "What is the next step? What now? What should I be doing?"

Location and Date of Creation

Virtual workshop, June 11, 2020

What Elements Went into the Sigil

- Enhance ability to listen, be receptive to and aware of opportunities
- Instill hope and positivity
- Foster acceptance/adaptability—to be flexible and willing to explore new options
- Provide illumination, increase visibility of path, encourage revelation
- Aid in releasing what's unneeded/holding you back
- Draw creativity and inspiration to you
- Encourage forward motion/mobility
- Maintain balance in a healthy manner

Clarity for the Next Step Sigil

Suggestions for Use

Use this sigil in scrying and divination, place it on your altar to act as a focal point, carve it into a candle (purple, green, blue, or white are all good options) to draw inspiration, anoint your body with it prior to trance or ritual working, or use it for meditation.

The Truth Speaks Sigil

Summary

This sigil is designed to fight misinformation, clearing the way for the truth to speak and be heard.

Location and Date of Creation

Virtual workshop, June 27, 2020

What Elements Went into the Sigil

- Revelation of truth
- Clarity/clear signal
- Movement of information in the correct direction
- Healing/health-focused
- Foster critical thinking/discernment
- Encourage positive action (things that help, not hurt)
- Community-mindful—being more conscious that we're all interconnected, to look out for everyone, not just the self
- Increase compassion and empathy

Suggestions for Use

Carve or place this sigil on a candle to help foster truth or direct the energy to community, local government, or media. Use it in protests to amplify the message or in scrying and divination to uncover what's blocking the truth as well as ward the truth.

The Truth Speaks Sigil

Wise Word Sigil

Wise Word Sigil

Summary

This sigil fosters clear and respectful communication, critical thinking, reading comprehension, and active listening.

Location and Date of Creation

Created by the author, Seattle, WA, September 13, 2018

What Elements Went into the Sigil

- Direct attention to the heart of the matter and the intent of the message/word
- Enhances the ability to understand what's being communicated
- Encourages new and creative thought patterns to increase comprehension
- Promotes balanced listening and learning, quieting the noise
- Interrupts feedback loops of a negative nature while aiding positive interaction
- Prevents knee-jerk, uninformed, disrespectful, and/or irrelevant responses
- Instills contemplation and deeper thinking

Suggestions for Use

Place this sigil on computers and phones and in classrooms and meeting rooms—places where communication takes place are ideal. Embed it in websites, emails, and signs.

Environmental Sigils

These sigils are focused on preserving and protecting the environment while also spreading awareness about climate change and issues affecting the health of our planet.

Adaptability Sigil (We Can Do It Sigil)

Summary

This sigil aids us in adapting to change in ways that will benefit both humankind and the planet. It helps us to be flexible in working toward creating a better society for all.

Adaptability Sigil

Location and Date of Creation

Virtual workshop, September 12, 2020

What Elements Went into the Sigil

- Resilience, protection
- Focus on climate change, personal responsibility, awareness
- Prepare for growth and becoming comfortable with a new normal
- Clarity and insight
- Peace, balance
- Reclaiming power, strength
- Healing

Suggestions for Use

Draw or carve this sigil on a candle (white, green, or blue is suggested), apply to the body with an oil that aligns with your focus, incorporate into workings focusing on climate change, use as a meditation focus, or use for the protection and guidance of body, home, and community.

Cool the Fires Sigil (for Land Connection and Healing)

Summary

This sigil helps us connect more deeply with the land to help prevent future fires and cool existing ones.

Cool the Fires Sigil

Location and Date of Creation

Virtual workshop, October 17, 2020

What Elements Went into the Sigil

- Land protection
- Encourage more favorable weather patterns
- Help with learning from the past/tapping into that wisdom to prevent future fires
- Stimulate belief in climate change and embrace science
- Safety for people, places, and animals
- Nurture the earth
- Soft rain (so the earth can soak/drink up the rain effectively)
- Balance
- Deepening connection/interconnection to the land

Suggestions for Use

Place this sigil on candles (basic white candles are fine; blue, green, or earth-colored candles are especially good), draw it in the earth around your home or in fire-vulnerable areas, use it as a meditation focus on your altar, or draw it on a map of affected areas to use as a focal point.

Containing Wildfires Sigil

Summary

This sigil can be used to help fight and contain raging wildfires, as well as put energy toward preventing uncontrolled fires.

Location and Date of Creation

The Green Man, Los Angeles, CA, November 9, 2018

What Elements Went into the Sigil

- Prevention
- Favorable weather patterns
- Awareness/education
- Emergency response/resources/support
- Protection
- Balance of environment

Containing Wildfires Sigil

Suggestions for Use

Carve this sigil into a candle (blue or green is recommended), place it in areas prone to fire to protect the land, draw it with water, or use it in meditation for weather ritual and magic.

Sigil to Protect Water

Summary

This sigil is designed to keep our water sources protected, clean, and free from corporate greed.

Location and Date of Creation

Earth Warriors Festival, Clarksville, OH, September 28, 2018

What Elements Went into the Sigil

- Clean water
- Accessible water
- Free-flowing water
- Free/no-cost water, no corporate interests
- Safeguard ground water
- Recognition of "as above, so below"
- Protection

Sigil to Protect Water

Suggestions for Use

Use this sigil with blue or white candles to send protection, draw it near bodies of water, direct it toward sources of pollution, or use it in conjunction with offerings to water spirits and deities.

Community Sigils

While the collection of sigils to protect people focuses on specific groups of people, the community sigils have a broader spectrum to help bring people together. They also focus on removing or alleviating the obstacles that prevent communion.

A Sigil to Build and Strengthen Community

Summary

This sigil is designed to help stimulate community through increased involvement, inclusion, awareness, understanding, and respect.

Location and Date of Creation

Fantasia Crystals, Phoenix, AZ, June 22, 2018

A Sigil to Build and
Strengthen Community

What Elements Went into the Sigil

- Enable a healthy flow of communication (speak/listen/acknowledge/understand)
- Emphasize mutual respect
- Help build a stable foundation and common ground
- Inspire dynamic/positive leadership
- Instill integrity
- Be inclusive, incorporating diversity
- Encourage participation/gathering

Suggestions for Use

This sigil is ideal for being placed in community spaces: drawn on walls and floors, made into altar cloths or flower arrangements, placed on banners, assembled at the base of a bonfire before it's lit, etc. It can be used to bless gatherings and festivals, Pagan Pride events, and so forth.

Common Ground Sigil

Summary

This sigil can help break down the barriers and preconceptions (and misconceptions) that prevent us from seeing that we have more in common with others than we may think.

Location and Date of Creation

Indigo Mermaid, Las Cruces, NM, November 5, 2018

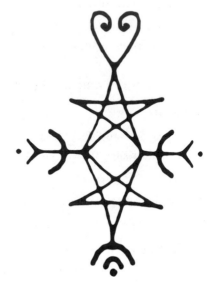

Common Ground Sigil

What Elements Went into the Sigil

- Letting go of the things that prevent us from finding common ground
- Improved communication
- Embracing the other
- Meeting halfway safely
- Adaptability
- Empathy
- Recognition of humanity
- Connection to earth/grounding

Suggestions for Use

You can use this sigil to lend support to others and bring more understanding, aid in conflict resolution, foster better communication at meetings and gatherings, or lift the veil from eyes that may otherwise be unable to look more deeply.

A Sigil for the Dissolution of Hate

Summary

The goal of the sigil is pretty much what it says: to dissolve hate. In order to move forward as a society, we have to clear and cleanse away hate—and that which breeds hatred.

Location and Date of Creation

Books, Beans & Candles, Birmingham, AL, October 28, 2018

What Elements Went into the Sigil

- Cleansing and purification of the spirit to remove hate
- Tolerance (of diversity, not of hate)
- Re-ordering of priorities for the good of all
- Forward movement
- Equal justice
- Self-love and love
- Education
- Power to change one's point of view, increase understanding
- Activate sympathy, empathy, and compassion
- Promote peace and harmony

Suggestions for Use

You can wear this sigil, share it, draw it in appropriate places, make signs of it, put it on candles, or use it for blessings and other forms of protection. You can use it to lend support to others and bring more understanding and to guide conflicts toward a positive and powerful solution.

A Sigil for the Dissolution of Hate

Equality Sigil

Summary

This sigil focuses on creating or rebuilding a community foundation based on equality, equity, and justice for all.

Location and Date of Creation

Thorn & Moon Magickal Market, Houston, TX, November 3, 2018

What Elements Went into the Sigil

Equality Sigil

- Generate unity
- Bring understanding
- Encourage love / compassion
- Instill patience
- Enable communication
- Build bridges
- Protect peace (warrior / guardian)

Suggestions for Use

This sigil can be placed in the heart of a town or city or a community gathering place, used in candle works (use whatever color seems appropriate for the area), directed toward legislation, or used as a focus for meditation.

Slice of the Pie Sigil

Summary

This sigil is designed to help create a society where everyone experiences abundance and is made to feel welcome.

Location and Date of Creation

Celestial Rites, Tucson, AZ, November 6, 2018

What Elements Went into the Sigil

- Prosperity and abundance
- Protection
- Inclusive, welcoming
- Self-perpetuating/building
- Love
- Acceptance/tolerance
- Healing

Slice of the Pie Sigil

Suggestions for Use

Use this sigil for demonstration signs, draw it in gathering places, or put it on a candle to help equalize a situation or bring an outcome that's equitable for all involved.

Root to Sky Sigil

Summary

This sigil encompasses the necessity of putting energy into the root of a situation so that the working may grow to address larger needs as it expands and resolves. It helps to get folks involved at the critical root level and keep the energy moving throughout the process—yielding more powerful long-term effects.

Root to Sky Sigil

Location and Date of Creation

Star + Splendor, Voorheesville, NY, September 24, 2019

What Elements Went into the Sigil

- Magnify/increase compassion
- Security/peace of mind for the people
- Support for the environment—especially in emphasizing leadership that fosters care and awareness for it
- Protection from fear (but also to be aware of what's happening—no fools)
- Engage/sustain community motivation
- Effective and timely justice

Suggestions for Use

This sigil is ideal for sharing and for group workings to support progress and positive growth in your local community and beyond. Put it on candles, use it for meditation, draw it on the ground, project it, or work it into legislation that affects your community. It helps to keep the flow of energy going—with motivation, relevance, a sense of peace, resolution, and security.

Transforming Anger Sigil

Summary

This sigil transforms anger so the end result is constructive and supportive, rather than directing that energy and creating violence.

Location and Date of Creation

Crystals, Candles & Cauldrons, Baltimore, MD, October 9, 2018

Transforming Anger Sigil

What Elements Went into the Sigil

- Encouraging constructive growth versus destructive action
- Space to be heard and acknowledged
- Providing resources and support
- Energy direction—disperses, dispels, or positively builds
- Cleansing
- Healing

Suggestions for Use

Place this sigil on candles with a focus on bringing peace and resolution to areas of conflict and violence. It can also be drawn on location at demonstrations and at other events susceptible to violence that could cause disruption or hide/hinder the message.

Voting and Election Sigils

These sigils are designed to protect voting rights. They acknowledge the relationship between metaphysical and mundane efforts. Both aspects are vital and necessary, helping to empower the people.

Bullseye Ballot Sigil

Summary

This sigil helps make sure your mail-in ballot gets delivered on time and gets counted.

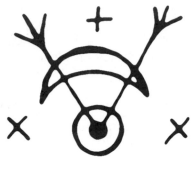

Location and Date of Creation

Created by the author, Rhode Island, October 10, 2020

What Elements Went into the Sigil

- Directly hitting the target (vote is received and counted)
- Making sure your vote/your voice is seen and included
- Ballot is protected from tampering or delays
- Encourages good health/truth/trust in the system
- Wards off negativity/bad intentions and reduces the power of those seeking to cause harm

Bullseye Ballot Sigil

To Draw This Sigil:

This sigil has a recommended order for drawing it on your ballot:

4. Draw a firm dot: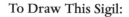
5. From the dot, draw a V (the dot being the base/crux of the V).
6. Draw a circle around the dot and base of the V.
7. On each arm of the V, draw a smaller V facing up to create the arrow tails/fletching.
8. Draw a crescent moon facing down that overlaps both arms.

9. Draw a + between the V arms, and place an X to the south, east, and west of the eye.

Suggestions for Use

It is vital that you fill out and return your mail-in ballot as soon as you receive it. Make sure to carefully follow the directions regarding the security envelope, signature, and postage (if required). This sigil can be easily and discreetly drawn on the inside flap of the outer envelope in the sticky area before you seal it. It will then become basically invisible and won't be seen by anyone once sealed *and* it will become part of the envelope. Don't draw the sigil on the outside of the envelope or anyplace else where it may be seen. If drawing the sigil so small isn't an option for you, you could also draw it with your finger on the envelope.

Election Protection Sigil

Summary

This sigil is designed to help safeguard an election from external tampering and to thwart those seeking to interfere with the democratic process.

Location and Date of Creation

Virtual workshop, October 22, 2020

What Elements Went into the Sigil

- Focus on community mental health/sanity
- Accessibility/end to voter repression/suppression
- Peaceful transition of power at all levels
- Fair and honest results quickly/truth empowered
- Freedom for all, benefiting the greater good, positive outcome
- Clarity and transparency
- Justice
- Protection from outside influences/tampering/obstruction
- Laying the groundwork leading to future progress/reunification/healing

Election Protection Sigil

Suggestions for Use

Draw or carve this sigil on a candle (white or blue is suggested) and burn it during the time when an election is taking place. Use this sigil to bless polling places and drop-off boxes (invisibly). You can adorn the body with it in subtle ways (if you're heading out to vote or working the polls).

Get Out and Vote Sigil

Summary

The name of this sigil says it all—the goal is to encourage people to participate in the voting process. Every vote does count. It reminds the voter not to be dissuaded by hype and not to let go of their right to be heard.

Location and Date of Creation

Atlanta Pagan Pride Day, October 20, 2018

What Elements Went into the Sigil

- Gets folks registered to vote in time
- Maximum effort/intent to vote
- Transportation/accessibility
- Safety
- Planning/make a plan
- Freedom to vote

Suggestions for Use

This sigil is ideal for use during voter registration drives. Put it in places where folks can register to vote or place it on candles to direct energy to folks who are eligible to vote.

Get Out and Vote Sigil

Protecting Voting Rights Sigil

Summary

This sigil smooths the way for the people to make their voices heard in the voting process without being hindered or restricted illegally or unjustly. It is especially handy for directing aid to areas where tampering, gerrymandering, voter intimidation, and other means of trying to disenfranchise or dissuade people from voting are very serious issues.

Protecting Voting Rights Sigil

Location and Date of Creation

Robin's Nest, Bellingham, MA, October 12, 2018

What Elements Went into the Sigil

- Awareness of voting rights
- Transparency of process
- Legal process
- Justice safeguarded
- Equality
- Accessibility for voting
- Authority, sovereign right upheld
- Fairness
- Protection

Suggestions for Use

This sigil can be used to protect polling places and locations where folks can register to vote, directed toward legislation affecting voting rights, or drawn on the skin with oil/worn discreetly for protection.

Living Democracy Sigil

Summary
This sigil is designed to help protect, promote, and preserve democracy.

Location and Date of Creation
Virtual workshop, January 16, 2021

What Elements Went into the Sigil

- Protection
- Keeping the peace
- Justice, fairness, accountability
- Freedom, light to/of liberty, illumination
- Truth revealed and the perspective to see it clearly and wholly
- Healing and resilience
- Integrity throughout
- Community, collaboration
- Promote respect and equality
- Future-focused, possibilities, potential, hope, prosper

Living Democracy Sigil

Design Notes
The sigil is printed here in black and white, but it is also published on my blog with a full-color version that is modeled after the Philadelphia Pride Flag.[44] I used the latter color scheme as inspiration, creating the color wheel around and placing brown and black in the center—between the two bars

---

44. Laura Tempest Zakroff, "The Living Democracy Sigil," *A Modern Traditional Witch* (blog), *Patheos*, January 16, 2021, https://www.patheos.com/blogs/tempest/2021/01/the-living-democracy-sigil.html.

that we use to symbolize integrity with equality combined. Without recognition of and respect for BIPOC voices, democracy cannot flourish.

Suggestions for Use

Use this sigil as a community focus in ritual, put it on a candle (white is a good basic color and blue is another excellent choice—follow your intuition), place it on your altar, use it in protection and justice-oriented spellcraft, add it to protest signs and shirts, or use it when working with deities who also represent democratic ideals and justice.

Combination Sigils

Usually, one sigil is more than enough to do the job, but occasionally multiple sigils can do the work better and more effectively than just one. Sometimes an issue is quite large or so complex in nature that breaking it down into smaller parts helps the problem be more easily addressed or solved. As the saying goes, many hands make light work. It's not that multiple sigils make a working any easier, but they can help us focus on integral, necessary aspects that may guide us to success more smoothly.

Included in this section are several kinds of combined sigils to give you different examples of when and how you might use a combination sigil or work multiple sigils together. As you'll see, all of the sigils within a combination or grouping are related, so they're still part of a common working versus being disparate or unrelated. The continuity builds momentum and crafts a stronger framework for success.

The Sevenfold Waning Moon Spell and Sigil is an example of a working that has multiple parts that can be used separately or combined together, depending on how much time and resources the user has.[45] I've also included the original instructions for the spell, so you can see how all the parts can work. The Quintisigil is a design utilizing five established sigils that you will recognize from earlier in this chapter. Each is present in its original form but has been arranged to make a new overall combined image harnessing the power of all five for different aspects. The next example may already be familiar to you if you've read my book *Anatomy of a Witch*. There are five individual sigils—one for each part of the Witch anatomy—and one larger sigil that combines them all. This approach allows you to focus on one system at a time and then address the whole body together. The Starbody Sigil was designed as a frontispiece to energetically represent the whole of a published work. The artwork utilizes both representative images and stylized sigils to bring forth its message.

---

45. This spell is explained in the following blog post and YouTube video: Laura Tempest Zakroff, "A Witch's Sevenfold Waning Moon Spell for Magical Resistance," *A Modern Traditional Witch* (blog), Patheos, June 6, 2020, www.patheos .com/blogs/tempest/2020/06/a-witchs-sevenfold-waning-moon-spell-for-magical-resistance.html; Laura Tempest Zakroff YouTube channel, "Sevenfold Waning Moon Spell—Magical Resistance," June 7, 2020, https://www.youtube .com/watch?v=UjLzqpW5hAc.

Sevenfold Waning Moon Spell and Sigil

Summary

The Sevenfold Waning Moon Spell is a magical resistance working designed to aid in breaking down and banishing systemic racism and destroying the white supremacy that feeds it. Every symbol part of the spell centers on a different aspect to be addressed and broken down. The spell is also designed to be flexible in terms of timing and application, so you can adapt it to fit your personal practice. Lots of folks tend to turn to the full moon for spellcasting, but every aspect of the lunar cycle can be utilized. The waning moon is an excellent time to work banishings, cleansings, and other workings that focus on diminishing or eroding issues. This spell is sevenfold because 7 is the number of the Chariot in the major arcana of the tarot, signifying forward momentum, conquest and triumph over enemies, and manifesting balance. Also, a lunar month is approximately 28 days, so this working is set for two weeks (half a lunar month), or the beginning, middle, and end of the waning moon period (7th, 14th, and 21st). Also, the Tower card is 16, or $1 + 6 = 7$.

Sevenfold Waning Moon Sigil
(*Left:* Individual Symbols
Right: Combined Sigil)

Date and Location of Creation

June 2020 (virtual release in a blog post and YouTube video)

What Elements Went into the Sigil

- Waning moon = Banish and release energy
- X = End police brutality and violence
- Eight-pointed asterisk = Erode ignorance and the misinformation that feeds racism

- Open eye = Remove protections that enable those who seek to harm and open blind eyes to their true actions so that true reform can happen
- Parallel wavy lines = Remove the bureaucracy that creates/upholds unjust laws
- Broken diamond with dots = Cut off money that supports systemic racism and redistribute it to community building
- Five-pointed star = Remove blockages to community advancement and growth
- Downward arrow = Destroy white supremacy

SYMBOLS OF THE
SEVENFOLD WANING MOON
MAGICAL RESISTANCE SPELL

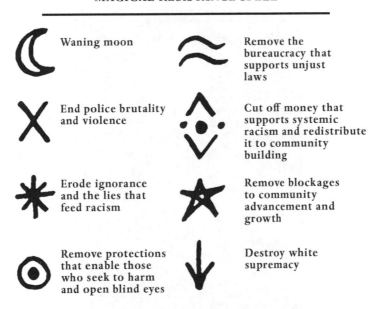

Symbols of the Sevenfold Waning Moon Spell

Two graphics are included with this spell. On the left is a line of eight symbols, so you can reference each one easily. On the right is the combined sigil that incorporates all of the symbols, if you have limited time or resources. The images could be printed out and pasted on a candle, but even if you do that, I recommend tracing/drawing over the symbols or sigil so you can really connect with it.

Supplies

- A seven-day candle, a tall taper candle, or 7 tealight candles (white or yellow)
- Candleholders (if needed)
- A marker or something to carve with
- A piece of paper or fabric (optional)

Sevenfold Waning Moon Candle

Directions

1. Take a candle long enough that you can mark out seven sections on it. This can be a tall seven-day candle in a glass jar or a tall taper. Suggested colors are white or yellow for clarity, cleansing, and justice, but choose what you are most drawn to for this working. With glass, you can paint or write on the holder with a permanent marker (black or purple is recommended for light-colored candles; you can use gold, yellow, or silver for dark candles). With a taper, you can carve or write on it. If you're completely out of tall candles, you can use seven tealights.

2. If your candle is wide enough at the top, draw a waning crescent moon on it around the wick. If your candle isn't wide enough, you can draw the waning moon on the bottom, on the taper holder, or on a piece of paper or fabric, and set it safely underneath. Then down the side of the candle, you will draw the next seven symbols. You can choose to draw them all at once, so you can see how long to burn the candle each evening, or you can draw the next symbol each night to get a fresh focus. With tealights, you can draw the waning moon on the bottom of each holder and the symbol on top. (Allow each tealight to burn out completely.)

3. As you light the candle, focus on what that symbol represents. If you work with a specific deity, spirit, or ancestor, you may call upon them to aid you in the task, such as "X, I call upon you and the powers of the waning moon to aid me in (the focus). May it be so." The focus is more important than words, so if you're inspired, you can sing, chant, dance—whatever is your preferred form of raising energy and guiding will in your practice. Allow the candle to burn through or past the symbol each evening.

4. The goal is to focus on one symbol each day for fourteen days (basically the length of time from the full moon to the new moon), so one tall candle per week (or one tealight per day). If you're unable to do this every day, then you can do the working in seven-day intervals using the combined sigil (see below), burning a whole candle each time.

How Does This Spell Work?

As with any spell, magic starts with thought. It helps turn attention to the crucial issues that need to be addressed. This working helps to direct focus and energy to what needs to be done—but it is not the only action you should be taking. As always, metaphysical action needs to be followed up with mundane or physical action, such as supporting local and national groups and organizations actively working for change, being invested and active in your local government, registering to vote and encouraging others to get out as well for *every* election, and following the guidance of community leaders.

Are There Any Suggested Deities or Spirits I Should Work With?

If you already work with deities or spirits, I recommend starting there. If you don't work with any currently, then focus on the divine presence within yourself, or call upon all of our common ancestors, or connect with members of the Mighty Dead (inspiring humans who have crossed over) who are associated with social justice. Do your research before calling upon any spirit or deity you've never worked with before, and introduce yourself prior to this working.

Can I Add Other Elements to This Spell?

Yes, do what you feel called to do as long as it's in line with the overall focus. For example, you might want to dress the candle in other ways, such as with oils, herbs, or other images. This spell can be a foundation for a larger working/ritual, or it can stand completely on its own. Embellishments are up to the individual Witch, magical practitioner, or coven.

Quintisigil

Summary

The Quintisigil (aka the Cinquesigil) represents the combined focus of five of the shared magic sigils that are most essential to dramatic social change. As this sigil incorporates five very powerful sigils, *quinti* refers to its fivefold nature and is also a play on the word *quintessential*. *Cinque* also refers to fivefold and is a nod to the herb cinquefoil, or five-finger grass, which has numerous magical properties assigned to it, including protection. The five points of the leaves are said to represent wisdom, power, health, money, and love. The sigils have been arranged with magical space in mind: four of them represent direction and elements, while the center connects above and below. All together, they create a crossroads where powerful magic can be worked.

Location and Date of Creation

This sigil was created in June 2020 in silkscreen collaboration with Little Black Egg in San Francisco, CA, to raise funds for Black Visions Collective, Juxtaposition Arts, Black Women Speak, National Bail Out, and Stacey Abrams's Fair Fight. The art was printed on shirts and patches. Over $5,500 was raised.

What Elements Went into the Combined Sigil

- *The Power Sigil (center):* The first of the shared magic sigils was created in November 2016. It is designed to protect and empower all those who need it, support human rights, and foster recognition of the other within each of us. The inverted variation of this sigil has been selected to foster community support at the root level.

- *A Sigil to Protect Protesters (east):* This sigil was designed not only to protect protesters but also to make sure their message is seen, visible, and heard and has impact—as well as to instill hope. The element of air is often associated with the east and is an element of communication.

- *The 2020 Freedom Sigil (south):* In the south, the direction often associated with the element of fire, this sigil represents freedom from the aging structures that bind and bend us—as individuals as well as a society and greater global community. It symbolizes freedom from corruption, inequality, bigotry, racism, and all the fears that impose upon basic human rights and dignity—as well as the health of the planet. It also represents freedom to help bring effective, lasting change that moves all of humanity forward without leaving anyone behind.

- *A Sigil for the Dissolution of Hate (west):* Using the cleansing and healing properties of elemental water, this sigil works to dissolve that which fosters hate. It creates the potential for fresh new ground that acts as a foundation of respect and understanding to be built up.

- *The Root to Sky Sigil (north):* Grounded in the element of earth, this sigil encompasses the necessity of putting energy into the root of a situation so that the working may grow to address larger needs as it expands and resolves. The sigil helps to get folks involved at that critical root level and keep the energy moving throughout the process—yielding more powerful long-term effects that benefit self, community, and beyond.

Quintisigil

Sigils from Anatomy of a Witch

Summary

In my book *Anatomy of a Witch*, I introduce five symbolic systems that connect to our magical practice and our bodies. There are the Witch Lungs, the Witch Heart, the Serpent, the Witch Bones, and the Weaver (or Witch Mind). Each has its own sigil for you to consider as you explore each system for yourself. You could draw them on your body or draw them on paper, wood, or stone to place on your altar. There's also a combined sigil that incorporates major design elements from each of the separate systems to represent the Witch's body as a whole. This image works well on a tall candle for altar work.

Date and Location of Creation

2019–2021, over the course of writing the book, which was released in June of 2021

What Elements Went into the Sigil

- *The Weaver:* mission control, higher connection, spirit, communication, the Cauldron of Wisdom, memory, nerve network, in balance with the body
- *Witch Lungs:* breath, exchange, interconnectivity, sovereignty, recognition of the invisible forces in our lives, awareness of personal/private versus public/permeable space, element of air
- *Witch Heart:* rhythm, ritual, patterns, inner vision, the Cauldron of Motion, inspiration, passion, finding your own drumbeat
- *Witch Bones:* structure, strength, tradition, ancestral connection, roots, cycles of life and death, spirits of place, connected movement
- *The Serpent:* primal self, intuition, the Cauldron of Warming, protection, creation, renewal, serpentine energy, fluidity, sensuality, healing

Left: Witch Anatomy Sigil
Right, from top to bottom: Weaver, Witch Lungs, Witch Heart, Witch Bones, Serpent

Starbody Sigil

Summary

The Starbody Sigil is a pen and ink drawing that was the basis for the frontispiece commissioned for Taschen's Library of Esoterica book *Witchcraft*, released in 2021. This design acknowledges that the elements of air, fire, water, earth, and spirit are present within our own bodies. We are a living crossroads of flesh and spirit, myth and mystery, inspiration and experience—made of star-stuff.

Location and Date of Creation

Summer 2021, New England

What Elements Went into the Sigil

Within this image we see sigils that represent the five elements, as well as more graphic representations of those elements in action. They are woven together to create a unified stellar body, much in the same way the book for which the sigil was designed brings together diverse ideas and traditions into a single collaborative exploration.

Suggestions for Use

The Starbody Sigil's primary purpose is to energetically represent the whole of a specific text, but it's also a tool for contemplation and personal exploration. Please note that unlike the shared magic sigils, the Starbody Sigil is not released under a creative commons license and is protected by traditional copyright (personal and licensed use). Therefore it cannot be reproduced in any way without my explicit permission.

Starbody Sigil

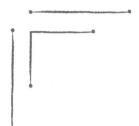

Conclusion

We have reached the end of this art journey together—for now. I hope you are inspired to make art and to look at the world with a little more magic in your eyes. Throughout this book I have included quotes from some of my favorite artists and creative folks. I'm finishing with one that I first read as a teenager, written by the poet Rainer Maria Rilke in a letter to his wife, the sculptor Clara Westhoff, in June of 1907. I have returned to his words again and again throughout my life, and this quote never ceases to take on new meaning for me with each successive reading:

> Surely all art is the result of one's having been in danger, of having gone through an experience all the way to the end, where no one can go any further. The further one goes, the more private, the more personal, the more singular an experience becomes, and the thing one is making is, finally, the necessary, irrepressible, and, as nearly as possible, definitive utterance of the singularity ... Therein lies the enormous aid the work of art brings to the life of the one who must make it.[46]

---

46. Rainer Maria Rilke, in a letter to his wife written on June 24, 1907, reprinted in *Letters on Cézanne*, edited by Clara Rilke, translated by Joel Agee (New York: North Point Press, 2002), 4.

When I was younger, I thought that the danger Rilke wrote about was the kind that comes from outside influences: physical harm, abusive situations, poverty, stress, etc. A couple (or more) decades later, I've come to realize that the danger comes from within us—our own fears and resistance to change. If we put aside our fears, we enter into a practice that harnesses the power and truth rooted within us, bringing it out for us and the world to see. To me, that is truly magic worth living and seeing.

Bibliography

Azéma, Marc, and Florent Rivère. "Animation in Palaeolithic Art: A Pre-echo of Cinema." *Antiquity* 86, no. 332 (June 2012): 316–24. https://doi.org/10.1017/S0003598X00062785.

Bantock, Nick. *The Artful Dodger: Images & Reflections.* San Francisco, CA: Chronicle Books, 2000.

Bayles, David, and Ted Orland. *Art & Fear: Observations on the Perils (and Rewards) of Artmaking.* Santa Cruz, CA: Image Continuum, 2001.

Boyd, Brian. *On the Origin of Stories: Evolution, Cognition, and Fiction.* Cambridge, MA: Belknap Press of Harvard University Press, 2009.

Cezzar, Juliette. *The AIGA Guide to Careers in Graphic and Communication Design.* New York: Bloomsbury, 2018.

Dutton, Denis. *The Art Instinct: Beauty, Pleasure, and Human Evolution.* New York: Bloomsbury Press, 2009.

Edwards, Betty. *The New Drawing on the Right Side of the Brain.* New York: Jeremy P. Tarcher/Putnam, 1999.

Flack, Audrey. *Art & Soul: Notes on Creating.* New York: Penguin Compass, 1986.

Gauger, Eliza. *Problem Glyphs.* Seattle, WA: Strix, 2017.

Gilbert, Elizabeth. *Big Magic: Creative Living Beyond Fear.* New York: Riverhead Books, 2015.

Gray, Martin Paul. "Cave Art and the Evolution of the Human Mind." MPhil thesis, Victoria University of Wellington, New Zealand, 2010. https://researcharchive.vuw.ac.nz/xmlui/handle/10063/1640.

Owl! at the Library (@SketchesbyBoze). Twitter, September 4, 2021, 10:24 p.m. https://twitter.com/SketchesbyBoze/status/1434356850737172481.

Ramachandran, V. S. *The Tell-Tale Brain: A Neuroscientist's Quest for What Makes Us Human*. New York: W. W. Norton, 2011.

Sopinka, Heidi. "An Interview with Leonora Carrington." The Believer, issue 94, November 1, 2012. https://believermag.com/an-interview-with-leonora-carrington-3.

Von Petzinger, Genevieve. *The First Signs: Unlocking the Mysteries of the World's Oldest Symbols*. New York: Atria Books, 2016.

Zakroff, Laura Tempest. *Anatomy of a Witch: A Map to the Magical Body*. Woodbury, MN: Llewellyn, 2021.

———. *Sigil Witchery: A Witch's Guide to Crafting Magick Symbols*. Woodbury, MN: Llewellyn, 2018.

———. *Weave the Liminal: Living Modern Traditional Witchcraft*. Woodbury, MN: Llewellyn, 2019.

———. "Witchual Workouts" playlist, Laura Tempest Zakroff YouTube channel. https://www.youtube.com/playlist?list=PL2TYo23upMtGqS-9RG4dtW8gHwdec3rAf.

Resources & Recommended Reading

Here are some additional suggestions to explore art and magic more:

Nonfiction

The Art of the Occult: A Visual Sourcebook for the Modern Mystic by S. Elizabeth

Austin Osman Spare: The Occult Life of London's Legendary Artist by Phil Baker

Drawing Blood by Molly Crabapple

The Hidden Geometry of Life: The Science and Spirituality of Nature by Karen L. French

Ithell Colquhoun: Genius of the Fern Loved Gully by Amy Hale

Magical Symbols and Alphabets: A Practitioner's Guide to Spells, Rites, and History by Sandra Kynes

Old in Art School: A Memoir of Starting Over by Nell Painter

Pan's Daughter: The Magical World of Rosaleen Norton by Nevill Drury

Women of the Golden Dawn: Rebels and Priestesses by Mary K. Greer

Wormwood Star: The Magickal Life of Marjorie Cameron by Spencer Kansa

Fiction

The Forgetting Room by Nick Bantock

Griffin and Sabine by Nick Bantock (seven books total)

The Hearing Trumpet by Leonora Carrington

The Honey Month by Amal El-Mohtar

Memory & Dream by Charles de Lint

My Name Is Asher Lev by Chaim Potok

The Wood Wife by Terri Windling

More Information about CC4 Licenses

The sigils found in Chapter 6: Sharing Sigils are covered by a Creative Commons Attribution-NonCommercial-ShareAlike 4.0 International License.[47] This means you are free to:

- **Share**—copy and redistribute the material in any medium or format
- **Adapt**—remix, transform, and build upon the material

The licensor cannot revoke these freedoms as long as you follow the license terms.

License terms:

- **Attribution**—You must give appropriate credit, provide a link to the license, and indicate if changes were made. You may do so in any reasonable manner, but not in any way that suggests the licensor endorses you or your use.
- **NonCommercial**—You may not use the material for commercial purposes.
- **ShareAlike**—If you remix, transform, or build upon the material, you must distribute your contributions under the same license as the original.
- **No additional restrictions**—You may not apply legal terms or technological measures that legally restrict others from doing anything the license permits.

Notices

You do not have to comply with the license for elements of the material in the public domain or where your use is permitted by an applicable exception or limitation.

No warranties are given. The license may not give you all of the permissions necessary for your intended use. For example, other rights such as publicity, privacy, or moral rights may limit how you use the material.

---

47. Creative Commons, "Attribution 4.0 International (CC BY 4.0)," https://creativecommons.org/licenses/by/4.0/.

To Write to the Author

If you wish to contact the author or would like more information about this book, please write to the author in care of Llewellyn Worldwide Ltd. and we will forward your request. Both the author and the publisher appreciate hearing from you and learning of your enjoyment of this book and how it has helped you. Llewellyn Worldwide Ltd. cannot guarantee that every letter written to the author can be answered, but all will be forwarded. Please write to:

Laura Tempest Zakroff
℅ Llewellyn Worldwide
2143 Wooddale Drive
Woodbury, MN 55125-2989

Please enclose a self-addressed stamped envelope for reply,
or $1.00 to cover costs. If outside the U.S.A., enclose
an international postal reply coupon.

Many of Llewellyn's authors have websites with additional information and resources. For more information, please visit our website at http://www.llewellyn.com.